CROCHETING PLACEMATS

Edited by
RITA WEISS

DOVER PUBLICATIONS, INC.
New York

American terminology, which is different from crochet terminology in most other parts of the world, is used for the stitches in this book. The following chart supplies the American name of crochet stitches and their equivalent in other countries. Crocheters should become thoroughly familiar with the differences in these terms before starting on any project.

AMERICAN NAME	EQUIVALENT
Chain	same
Slip	Single crochet
Single crochet	Double crochet
Half-double or short-double crochet	Half-treble crochet
Double crochet	Treble crochet
Treble crochet	Double-treble crochet
Double-treble crochet	Treble-treble crochet
Treble-treble or long-treble crochet	Quadruple-treble crochet
Afghan stitch	Tricot crochet

Published in Canada by General Publishing Company, Ltd., 30 Lesmill Road, Don Mills, Toronto, Ontario.
Published in the United Kingdom by Constable and Company, Ltd., 10 Orange Street, London WC2H 7EG.

This Dover edition, first published in 1978, is a new selection of patterns from *Doilies, Luncheon Sets, Table Runners* by Carolyn Graeves, published by the Spool Cotton Company in 1940; *Doilies* by Carolyn Graeves, published by the Spool Cotton Company in 1942; *Hand Crochet by Royal Society,* published by Royal Society, Inc., in 1945; *Hand Crochet Decorations,* published by Bernhard Ulmann Company, Inc., in 1937; *Doilies, Luncheon Sets and Table Runners* by Carolyn Graeves, published by the Spool Cotton Company in 1938; *Crocraft for Cynthia Mercerized Crochet Cottons, Book No. 50,* published by Cynthia Mills (n.d.); *Crocraft for Cynthia Mercerized Crochet Cottons, Book No. 51,* published by Cynthia Mills (n.d.); *The Table Cloth Book: Crochet Designs* by Cecilia Vanek, published by the American Thread Company (n.d.); *Flower Doilies and a New Pansy Doily,* published by the American Thread Company in 1949; *Bucilla Cotton Crochet Creations, Volume 117,* published by Bernhard Ulmann Company, Inc., in 1937; *Old and New Favorites. Doilies* by E. L. Mathieson, published by the Spool Cotton Company in 1946.

International Standard Book Number: 0-486-23700-1
Library of Congress Catalog Card Number: 78-56777

Manufactured in the United States of America
Dover Publications, Inc.
180 Varick Street
New York, N.Y. 10014

INTRODUCTION

It has often been said that a hostess is judged by the table she sets. As your guests enter your dining room, the first thing they see is the dining room table; everything else tends to recede into the background. You may have the most delightful pictures on the wall, the richest rugs underfoot, the most impressive draperies at the window. They all play important roles in the decorative scheme, but the attention of your guests is irresistibly focused on the table. And there is nothing more gracious on the table than a beautifully hand-crocheted set of placemats.

This is a new collection of some of the most lovely crocheted placemat patterns published in instruction brochures over thirty years ago, during a period when the making of hand-crocheted lace was an extremely popular pastime. Today, as we return once again to the joys of creating exquisite handmade articles, the crocheting of placemats for the table is enjoying a new surge of popularity.

A set of crocheted placemats is a real investment in beauty because it wears practically forever, remaining a classic long after other table fashions have come and gone. Best of all, crocheted lace has the elusive, intrinsic quality that comes with handmade things. A novice in the art of the crochet hook can learn her first lesson fashioning a beautiful placemat; a master crocheter can work up the more elaborate ideas to display her skill.

Although most of the threads listed with the patterns are still available, you may wish to substitute some of the newer cottons, synthetics and polyesters now on the market. Check with your local needlework shop or department. Whatever type of thread you decide to use, be certain to buy at one time sufficient thread of the same dye lot to complete the set of placemats you wish to make. It is often impossible to match shades later as dye lots vary.

For perfect results the number of stitches and rows should correspond with that indicated in the directions. Before starting your placemat, make a small sample of the stitch, working with the suggested needle size and desired thread. If your working tension is too tight or too loose, use a coarser or finer crochet hook to obtain the correct gauge.

When you have completed your placemats, they should be washed and blocked before using them. No matter how carefully you have worked, blocking will improve a placemat's appearance and give it a "professional" look. Use a good neutral soap or detergent and make suds in warm water. Wash by squeezing the suds through the placemat, but do not rub. Rinse two or three times in clear water and squeeze out the excess water. Following the measurements given with the pattern, and using rust-proof pins, pin the article right side down on a well-padded, flat surface. Be sure to pin out all picots, loops, scallops, etc., along the outside edges. When the placemat is almost completely dry, press through a damp cloth with a moderately hot iron (do not rest the iron on the decorative, raised stitches). When thoroughly dry, remove the pins.

All of the stitches and abbreviations used in the projects in this book are explained on page 48.

MODERN SQUARES

This luncheon set is news! Smart squares of serene beauty that grace a luncheon table of modern or period feeling with equal charm.

MATERIALS: For best results use—
CLARK'S O.N.T. OR J. & P. COATS
BEST SIX CORD MERCERIZED CROCHET, Size 30:
SMALL BALL:
CLARK'S O.N.T.—*13 balls of White or Ecru, or 20* OR *balls of any color.*
J. & P. COATS—*10 balls of White or Ecru, or 13 balls of any color.*
BIG BALL:
CLARK'S O.N.T.—*5 balls of White or Ecru.*
OR
J. & P. COATS—*5 balls of White or Ecru, or 7 balls of any color.*
MILWARD'S *steel crochet hook No. 10.*

These materials are sufficient for a set consisting of a centerpiece about 15" x 15"; 4 place doilies about 12" x 12"; 4 bread and butter plate doilies about 8" x 8"; and 4 glass doilies about 5" x 5".

GAUGE: 5 small sps make 1 inch; 5 short rows make 1 inch. 5 large sps make 2 inches; 5 long rows make 2 inches.

Center filet section of each doily is worked first; the large sps in corners are worked in afterwards.

CENTERPIECE *(Center Section)*... Starting at "A" ch 48 (15 ch sts to 1 inch). **1st row:** D c in 4th ch from hook, d c in next 2 ch (1 bl made). * Ch 2, skip 2 ch, d c in next ch (1 sp made). Repeat from * 12 more times (13 sps); d c in next 3 ch. Ch 3, turn.

2nd row: D c in next 3 d c, * ch 2, d c in next d c. Repeat from * 12 more times, d c in last 2 d c and in 3rd st of turning ch. Ch 8, turn. **3rd row:** D c in 4th ch from hook, d c in next 4 ch (2 bls increased). D c in next 4 d c, 13 sps, d c in next 2 d c; then make a foundation d c as follows: *Thread over, insert hook in top st of turning ch and draw a loop through; thread over and draw through 1 loop (1 ch st made, to be used as a foundation st for next d c); complete d c in usual way.* Make 5 more foundation d c, and 1 d c in the usual way (2 bls increased). Ch 3, turn. **4th row:** D c in next 3 d c; (ch 2, skip 2 d c, d c in next d c) twice; (ch 2, skip 2 ch, d c in next d c) 13 times; (ch 2, skip 2 d c, d c in next d c) twice; d c in last 3 d c. Ch 8, turn. **5th row:** Make 2 bls over turning ch-8 as before; 1 bl over next bl, 17 sps, d c in next 2 d c, foundation d c in turning ch; then inc. 2 bls at end of row. Ch 3, turn. **6th row:** 1 bl, 5 sps; (2 d c in next sp, d c in next d c) twice—*2 bls made:* 3 sps, 1 bl, 3 sps, 2 bls, 5 sps, 1 bl. Ch 8, turn. Now follow chart for centerpiece, starting at 7th row, until 45 rows are made. Ch 1 to turn at end of 45th row. **46th row:** Sl st in each st of 1st 2 bls, ch 3 and follow chart across to within 2 bls from end, ch 3, turn (2 bls decreased). Follow chart to top. Fasten off.

First Corner... Join thread at "B", ch 99 (15 ch sts to 1 inch); turn. **1st row:** D tr in 16th ch from hook, * ch 5, skip 5 ch, d tr in next ch (2 large sps made). Repeat from * 12 more times, join with sl st to base of turning ch of 3rd row of center section (15 large sps). **2nd row:** Sl st along side of 3rd and 4th rows of center and along bottom of next 2 bls of 5th row, turn; skip 5 ch, d tr in next d tr, * ch 5, d tr in next d tr. Repeat from * 11 more times, ch 5, skip 5 ch, d tr in next ch (14 large sps). Ch 10, turn. Now follow chart until 14 rows of large sps are made; then make a d tr in base of turning ch of 31st row of center section. Fasten off. Make other 3 corners in same way. Work 1 row of s c completely around, keeping work flat. Fasten off.

PLACE DOILIES *(Make 4)* **... Center Section...** Starting at "A", ch 42 and work filet center as for centerpiece, following place doily chart. To make corners, join thread at "B", ch 81, d tr in 16th ch from hook, and work as before. Work 1 row of s c completely around.

BREAD AND BUTTER PLATE DOILIES *(Make 4)* **... Center Section...** Starting at "A", ch 18 and work filet center as for centerpiece, following chart for bread and butter plate doily. To make corners, join thread at "B", ch 63, d tr in 16th ch from hook, and work as before. Work 1 row of s c completely around.

GLASS DOILIES *(Make 4)* **... Center Section...** Starting at "A", ch 30 and work filet center as for centerpiece, following glass doily chart. To make corners, join thread at "B", ch 33, d tr in 16th ch from hook and work as before. Work 1 row of s c completely around.

CHARTS FOR "MODERN SQUARES"

CENTERPIECE

PLACE DOILY

BREAD & BUTTER PLATE DOILY

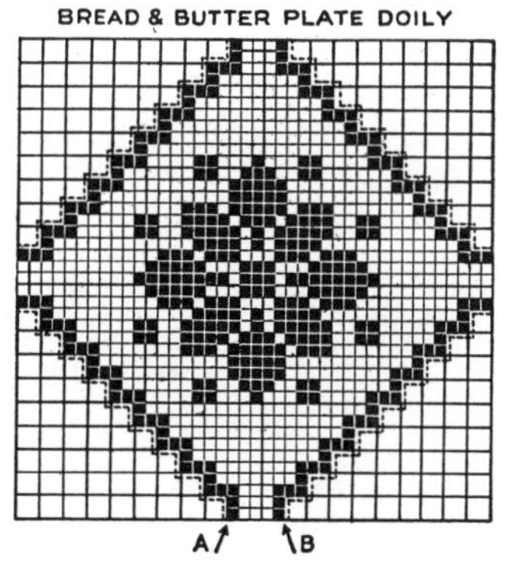

GLASS DOILY

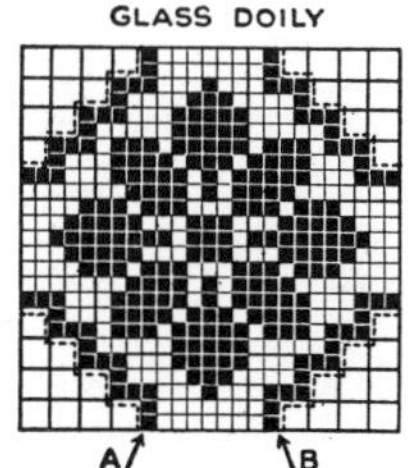

CRISS CROSS Handsome latticework frames the solid smart centers.

MATERIALS: For best results use—
CLARK'S O.N.T. OR J. & P. COATS
BEST SIX CORD MERCERIZED CROCHET, Size 10:
SMALL BALL:
CLARK'S O.N.T.—*22 balls of White or Ecru.*
OR
J. & P. COATS—*16 balls of White or Ecru.*
BIG BALL:
CLARK'S O.N.T. OR J. & P. COATS—*9 balls of White or Ecru.*
MILWARD'S *steel crochet hook No. 9.*
Set consists of 4 place mats, each about 12½ x 16 inches, and a center mat about 16 x 30 inches.
GAUGE: 9 sts make 1 inch; 3 s c-rows and 2 tr-rows make 1 inch.

PLACE MATS *(Make 4)*... Starting at solid section, make a 15-inch chain (9 ch sts to 1 inch). **1st row:** Tr in 5th ch from hook and in each ch across until there are 108 tr, counting turning ch as 1 tr (about 12 inches). Cut off remaining chain. Ch 1, turn. **2nd row:** S c in each tr across. Ch 4 (to count as 1st tr of next row), turn. **3rd row:** Tr in each s c across. Ch 1, turn. Repeat 2nd and 3rd rows alternately until piece measures 8½ inches, ending with an s c-row. Do not break off. Work s c along remaining 3 sides, making 3 s c at corners; join with sl st. Sl st in next 2 s c and work border as follows:

1st rnd: Ch 5; make 2 d tr at base of ch-5, retaining on hook last loop of each d tr; thread over and draw through all loops on hook (cluster). * Skip 6 s c; 2 d tr in next s c, retaining on hook last loop of each d tr; thread over and draw through all loops on hook; ch 5, s c where last 2 d tr were made (another cluster); ch 5 and complete a cluster as before at base of this ch-5. Repeat from * around, working an extra cluster-group at each corner to keep following rows flat. Join ch-5 of last cluster with sl st to base of 1st cluster. **2nd rnd:** Sl st in each st of ch-5 of 1st cluster, s c at tip of 2-cluster group, ch 5, d tr in same place as last s c. * Ch 5, s c at base of this tr (thus completing cluster), ch 5, complete cluster as on previous row with 2 d tr at base of ch-5; 2 d tr (worked off as 1 st) at tip of next cluster-group. Repeat from * around; join last cluster to tip of 1st one with an s c. **3rd rnd:** * Ch 5, s c in last s c made; ch 12, s c between next 2 joined clusters. Repeat from * around, joining last ch-12 to base of 1st ch-5. **4th rnd:** Sl st in ch-5 loop, ch 5. Make 2 d tr (worked off as 1 st) to complete beginning cluster. * Ch 5, s c in 3rd st from hook (thus making ch-2 and p), ch 2, make 3-d tr cluster in same loop by working off 3 d tr as 1 st and making ch-1 to fasten cluster. Repeat from * once (this is corner loop). ** S c in next ch-12 loop, ch 1; in next ch-5 loop make two 3-d tr clusters separated by (ch-2, p and ch-2). Repeat from ** around, making 3 clusters in the 2 corner loops to keep work flat. Fasten off.

CENTER MAT... Work solid section exactly as for place mats, but work for 26 (instead of 8½) inches. Then work cluster edging all around.

AMERICANA

From coast to coast, women will crochet this seven-piece luncheon set, for it has the simplicity and charm that fit so well into the American home!

MATERIALS: Use one of the following threads—

J. & P. COATS KNIT-CRO-SHEEN, *7 balls of White or Ecru, or 8 balls of any color.*

CLARK'S O.N.T. LUSTERSHEEN, *5 skeins of White or Ecru, or 7 skeins of any color.*

MILWARD'S *steel crochet hook No. 4 or 5.*

When blocked, place mats measure about 12 x 18 inches; center mat measures about 12 x 32 inches.

GAUGE: 4 rows make 1¾ inches.

PLACE MATS *(Make 6)* ...Starting at short side, make a 16-inch chain (11 ch sts to 1 inch). **1st row:** Tr in 5th ch from hook, tr in next 3 ch, * ch 3, skip 3 ch, tr in next ch, ch 3, skip 3 ch, tr in next 5 ch. Repeat from * across until 10 tr-groups are made, ending with 5 tr. Cut off remaining chain. Ch 8, turn. **2nd row:** * Skip 3 tr, tr in last tr of tr-group, ch 3, make a cluster in next tr—*to make a cluster, make 4 tr, retaining on hook the last loop of each tr; thread over and draw through all loops; ch 1 tightly*—ch 2 more, tr in next tr, ch 3. Repeat from * across, ending with ch 3, tr in 4th st of turning ch. Ch 4, turn. **3rd row:** * Tr in each of 3 ch, tr in next tr; in tip of cluster make tr, ch 9 and tr; tr in next tr. Repeat from * across, ending with tr in 1st 4 ch of ch-8. Ch 4, turn. **4th row:** Tr in next 4 tr, * ch 3, s c in ch-9 loop, ch 3, tr in next 5 tr. Repeat from * across (last tr is made in turning ch). Ch 8, turn. **5th row:** Like 2nd row (making clusters in s c of previous row). **6th row:** * Tr in next 3 ch, tr in next tr, ch 3, tr in tip of cluster; ch 3, tr in next tr. Repeat from * across, ending with tr in 4th st of turning ch. Ch 8, turn. Repeat 2nd to 6th rows incl. until piece measures approximately 16½ inches. Do not break off but, keeping work flat, make s c all around. Then make another row of s c, picking up back loop only. Fasten off.

CENTER MAT...Work as for place mats until piece measures approximately 29½ inches (instead of 16½). Then work 2 rows of s c as for place mats. Fasten off.

Block pieces to given measurements.

Enhance your luncheon table by crocheting these delightful settings for hospitality!

Marlborough

MATERIALS:

CLARK'S O.N.T. or J. & P. COATS BEST SIX CORD MERCERIZED CROCHET, size 50:

CLARK'S O.N.T.—11 balls of White or Ecru, or 14 balls of color,

OR

J. & P. COATS —7 balls of White or Ecru.

Steel crochet hook No. 13.

This amount of material is sufficient for a set consisting of a centerpiece, 14 inches in diameter; 4 plate doilies, 11 inches in diameter; 4 bread and butter plate doilies, 7½ inches in diameter, and 4 glass doilies, 5 inches in diameter.

CENTERPIECE . . . Ch 10, join with sl st. **1st rnd:** Ch 4, 29 tr in ring, sl st in 4th st of ch-4. **2nd rnd:** Ch 4, tr in same place as sl st, 2 tr in each tr around. Sl st in 4th ch. **3rd rnd:** Ch 4, tr in each tr around, sl st in 4th ch. **4th rnd:** Ch 5, * tr in next tr, ch 1. Repeat from * around. Sl st in 4th st of ch-5. **5th rnd:** Ch 6, * tr in next tr, ch 2. Repeat from * around. Sl st in 4th st of ch-6. **6th rnd:** Sc in 1st ch-2 sp, ch 6, sc in 4th ch from hook (p), ch 3, p, * ch 2, skip 2 sps, sc in next sp, ch 2, p, ch 3, p. Repeat from * around, ending with ch 2, skip 2 sps, sl st in 1st sc. **7th rnd:** Sl st in 1st 3 sts of next loop, sl st in loop, ch 4, 2 tr in same loop, * ch 3, 3 tr in same loop, ch 3, 6 tr in center of next loop, ch 3, 3 tr in next loop. Repeat from * around, ending with ch 3, sl st in 4th st of ch-4. **8th rnd:** Sl st in next 2 tr, sl st in ch-3 sp, ch 4, 2 tr in same sp, * ch 3, 3 tr in same sp, ch 4, tr in 6 tr, ch 4, skip 1 sp, 3 tr in next sp. Repeat from * around, ending with ch 4. Join. **9th rnd:** Sl st in next 2 tr, sl st in ch-3 sp, ch 4, 2 tr in same sp, ch 3, 3 tr in same place (shell over shell made—1st shell at beginning of the following rnds is made in the same manner), * ch 4, (tr in next tr, ch 1) 5 times; tr in next tr, ch 4, in next ch-3 sp make 3 tr, ch 3 and 3 tr (another shell made). Repeat from * around, ending with ch 4. Join. **10th rnd:** * Shell over shell, ch 5, (tr in next tr, ch 1) 5 times; tr in next tr, ch 5. Repeat from * around. Join. **11th rnd:** * Shell over shell, ch 5, (tr in next ch-1 sp, ch 4) 4 times; tr in next ch-1 sp, ch 5. Repeat from * around. Join. **12th rnd:** * Shell over shell, ch 6, (tr in next ch-4 loop, ch 5) 3 times; tr in next loop, ch 6. Repeat from * around. Join. **13th rnd:** * Shell over shell, ch 7, (tr in next ch-5 loop, ch 6) twice; tr in next loop, ch 7. Repeat from * around. Join. **14th rnd:** * Shell over shell, ch 11, tr in ch-6 loop, ch 6, tr in next loop, ch 11. Repeat from * around. Join. **15th rnd:** Sl st in next 2 tr, sl st in next ch, sc in sp, * (ch 2, ch-4 p) twice; ch 1 (p-loop made), sc in ch-11 loop, make another p-loop, sc in same loop; make another p-loop, sc in next sp. Repeat from * around. Fasten off.

16th rnd: Petals are made individually as follows: **First Petal: 1st row:** Starting at center, ch 10, sc in 3rd ch from hook and in each of next 6 ch, 3 sc in last ch, and working along opposite side of foundation ch make sc in next 7 ch, sc in turning ch, ch 2, turn. Hereafter pick up only the back loop of each sc throughout. **2nd to 5th rows incl:** Skip 1 sc, sc in each sc to center of 3 sc group, 3 sc in center sc, sc in each sc across, sc in turning ch. Ch 2, turn. **6th row:** Skip 1 sc, sc in each sc to center sc at base of petal, sc in center of p-loop on 15th rnd, sc in same place as last sc on petal, sc in each sc across, sc in turning ch. Fasten off. **Second Petal: 1st to 5th rows incl:** Repeat 1st to 5th rows of 1st petal, ending with ch 1. **6th row:** Sl st in last sc of 1st petal, ch 1, skip 1 sc, and complete as for 1st petal joining base of petal as before to 2nd loop following the one where 1st petal was joined. Work in this manner around, always joining petals to previous one and to loops on 15th rnd always skipping a loop between petals. Join last petal to 1st petal made. Do not fasten off at end of rnd. **17th rnd:** Sc between two petals, * make a p-loop, skip 3 rows of petal, sc in next row, make another p-loop, skip 4 rows of petal, sc in next row, make another p-loop, sc in sp between petals. Repeat from * around. **18th and 19th rnds:** Sl st to center of loop, * make a p-loop, sc in center of next p-loop. Repeat from * around. Fasten off at end of 19th rnd. **20th rnd:** Work as for 16th rnd but having 8 rows of sc on each petal (instead of 6 rows) and skipping 2 loops (instead of one loop) when joining to previous rnd. **21st rnd:** Sc between two petals, * make a p-loop, skip 3 rows of petal, sc in next row, make a p-loop, skip 4 rows of petal, sc in foundation ch of petal, make a p-loop, skip 4 rows of petal, sc in next row, make a p-loop, skip 3 rows of petal, sc between petals. Repeat from * around. **22nd to 26th rnd:** Repeat 18th rnd, ending last rnd with sl st in center of first p-loop.

PLACE MATS (Make 4) . . . Work as for Centerpiece to 19th rnd incl. Then work 2 more rnds of loops as before. Fasten off.

BREAD and BUTTER PLATE DOILY (Make 4) . . . Work as for Centerpiece to 10th rnd incl. **11th rnd:** Sl st to sp, * ch 2, p, ch 3, p, ch 2, sc in

(continued on page 10)

Flower Spoke

MATERIALS:

CLARK'S O.N.T. or J. & P. COATS BEST SIX CORD MERCERIZED CROCHET, size 30:

SMALL BALL:
CLARK'S O.N.T.—11 balls,
OR
J. & P. COATS —7 balls of White or Ecru, or 9 balls of any color.

BIG BALL:
J. & P. COATS —4 balls of White or Ecru, or 5 balls of any color.

Steel crochet hook No. 10 or 11.

This amount of material is sufficient for a set consisting of a centerpiece, 14 inches in diameter; 4 place doilies, 11 inches in diameter; 4 bread and butter plate doilies, 6½ inches in diameter, and 4 glass doilies, 4½ inches in diameter.

CENTERPIECE . . . Starting at center, ch 10. Join. **1st rnd:** Ch 4 (to count as tr), 23 tr in ring, sl st in 4th st of ch-4. **2nd rnd:** Ch 4, tr in same place as sl st, * ch 7, skip 3 tr, 2 tr in next tr. Repeat from * around. Join last ch-7 to 4th st of ch-4. **3rd rnd:** Ch 4, tr in same place as sl st, * ch 5, 2 tr in next tr. Repeat from * around. Join. **4th rnd:** Ch 4, tr in same place as sl st, * ch 3, 2 tr in next tr. Repeat from * around. Join. **5th rnd:** Ch 4, tr in next tr, * ch 5, tr in next 2 tr, ch 3, tr in next 2 tr. Repeat from * around. Join. **6th rnd:** Ch 4, tr in next tr, * ch 3, tr in same place as last tr, tr in next tr, ch 3, tr in same place as last tr, tr in next tr, ch 3, tr in next 2 tr. Repeat from * around. Join. **7th rnd:** Ch 4, tr in next tr, * ch 3, tr in same place as last tr, skip next tr, tr in next tr, tr in next tr, ch 3, tr in same place as last tr, tr in next tr, ch 3, tr in next 2 tr. Repeat from * around. Join. **8th rnd:** Ch 4, * 2 tr in next tr, ch 3, tr in same place as last tr, skip next tr, tr in next tr, skip next tr, tr in next tr, ch 3, 2 tr in same tr as last tr was made, tr in next tr, ch 3, tr in next tr. Repeat from * around. Join. **9th rnd:** Ch 4, tr in next 2 tr, * ch 4, tr in same place as last tr, (skip next tr, tr in next tr) twice; ch 4, tr in same place as last tr, tr in next 2 tr, ch 3, tr in next 3 tr. Repeat from * around. Join. **10th rnd:** Ch 4, tr in next 2 tr, * ch 5, d tr in same place as last tr, skip next st, tr in next tr, skip next st, d tr in next tr, ch 5, tr in same place as last d tr, tr in next 2 tr, ch 3, tr in next 3 tr. Repeat from * around. Join. **11th to 20th rnds:** Repeat the 10th rnd, having 2 additional sts in ch bars (between 3 tr groups) in each successive rnd, thus increasing 24 ch's in each rnd. There should be 23 ch's between the tr groups on the 20th rnd.

21st rnd: Ch 4, tr in next 2 tr, * in next tr make tr, ch 5 and tr; tr in next 3 tr, ch 13, in center st of next ch make sc, ch-9 and sc; ch 13, tr in next 3 tr. Repeat from * around. Join. **22nd rnd:** Ch 4, tr in next 2 tr, * ch 1, tr in ch-5 sp, ch 1, tr in next 3 tr, ch 7, in ch-9 loop make 21 d tr, ch 7, tr in next 3 tr. Repeat from * around. Join. **23rd rnd:** Ch 4, tr in next 2 tr, tr in the 3 tr of next tr group, ** ch 7, * d tr in next 3 d tr, ch 3. Repeat from * 5 more times; d tr in next 3 d tr, ch 7, tr in each tr of next two 3 tr groups. Repeat from ** around. Join. **24th rnd:** Ch 4, holding back the last loop of each tr make tr in next 5 tr, thread over and draw through all loops on hook (tr cluster made), ** ch 9, holding back on hook the last loop of each d tr, make * d tr in next 3 d tr, thread over and draw through all loops on hook (d tr cluster made), ch 10. Repeat from * 5 more times; make a cluster over remaining 3 sts of this group, ch 9 and work a tr cluster over the next 6 tr. Repeat from ** around. Join and fasten off.

PLACE DOILY (Make 4) . . . Work as for Centerpiece to 17th rnd incl. **18th rnd:** Ch 4, tr in next 2 tr, * in next tr make tr, ch 5 and tr; tr in next 3 tr, ch 10, in center st of ch-17 make sc, ch 7 and sc; ch 10, tr in next 3 tr. Repeat from * around. Join. **19th rnd:** Ch 4, tr in next 2 tr, * ch 1, tr in ch-5 sp, ch 1, tr in next 3 tr, ch 7, in ch-7 loop make 15 d tr; ch 7, tr in next 3 tr. Repeat from * around. Join. **20th rnd:** Ch 4, holding back on hook the last loop of each tr make tr in next 2 tr and in the 3 tr of next tr group and work together as a cluster, ** ch 7, * make a 3-d tr cluster over next 3 d tr, ch 10. Repeat from * 3 more times; make a cluster over remaining 3 sts of this group, ch 7, work a tr cluster over the 6 tr of next 2 tr groups as before. Repeat from ** around. Join and fasten off.

BREAD AND BUTTER DOILY (Make 4) . . . Work as for Centerpiece to 9th rnd incl. **10th rnd:** Ch 4, tr in next 2 tr, * skip next tr, in next tr make tr, ch 3 and tr; skip next tr, tr in next 3 tr, ch 3, 5 d tr in next sp, ch 3, tr in next 3 tr. Repeat from * around. Join. **11th rnd:** Ch 4, holding back on hook the last loop of each tr, make tr in next 2 tr, skip next 2 tr, tr in next 3 tr, thread over and draw through all loops on hook, * ch 7, holding back on hook the last loop of each d tr make 3 d tr in next d tr, thread over and draw through all loops on hook (cluster made); (ch 7, in next d tr make a 3-d tr cluster) 4 times; ch 7, holding back on hook the last loop of each tr, tr in next 3 tr, skip 2 tr, tr in next 3 tr, thread over and draw through all loops on hook. Repeat from * around. Join.

(continued on page 10)

Marlborough

(continued from page 8)

next sp, ch 2, p, ch 3, p, ch 2, skip 1 dc, sc in next dc, ch 2, p, ch 3, p, ch 2, skip 2 dc, sc in next dc, ch 2, p, ch 3, p, ch 2, sc in next sp, ch 2, p, ch 3, p, ch 2, sc in sp of next shell. Repeat from * around. Now repeat 16th to 19th rnds incl of Centerpiece. Fasten off.

GLASS DOILY (Make 4) . . . Work as for Centerpiece to 6th rnd incl, skipping 3 (instead of 2) sps under each loop on the 6th rnd. **7th rnd:** Work petals as for 16th rnd of Centerpiece, joining a petal to center of each loop. **8th, 9th and 10th rnds:** Repeat 17th, 18th and 19th rnds of Centerpiece. Fasten off.

FlowerSpoke

(continued from page 9)

GLASS DOILY (Make 4) . . . Work as for Centerpiece to 6th rnd incl. **7th rnd:** Ch 4, tr in next tr, * skip 1 tr, in next tr make tr, ch 3 and tr; tr in next 2 tr, ch 3, 3 d tr in next sp, ch 3, tr in next 2 tr. Repeat from * around. Join. **8th rnd:** Ch 4, holding back on hook the last loop of each tr make tr in next tr, skip next 2 tr, tr in next 2 tr, thread over and draw through all loops on hook, * (ch 7, make a d tr cluster in next d tr) 3 times; ch 7, holding back the last loop of each tr make tr in next 2 tr, skip 2 tr, tr in next 2 tr, thread over and draw through all loops on hook. Repeat from * around. Join. Starch lightly and press.

Chatelaine

CHARTS FOR DIRECTIONS ON OPPOSITE PAGE

There are 10 spaces between heavy lines

GLASS MAT

BREAD & BUTTER PLATE MAT

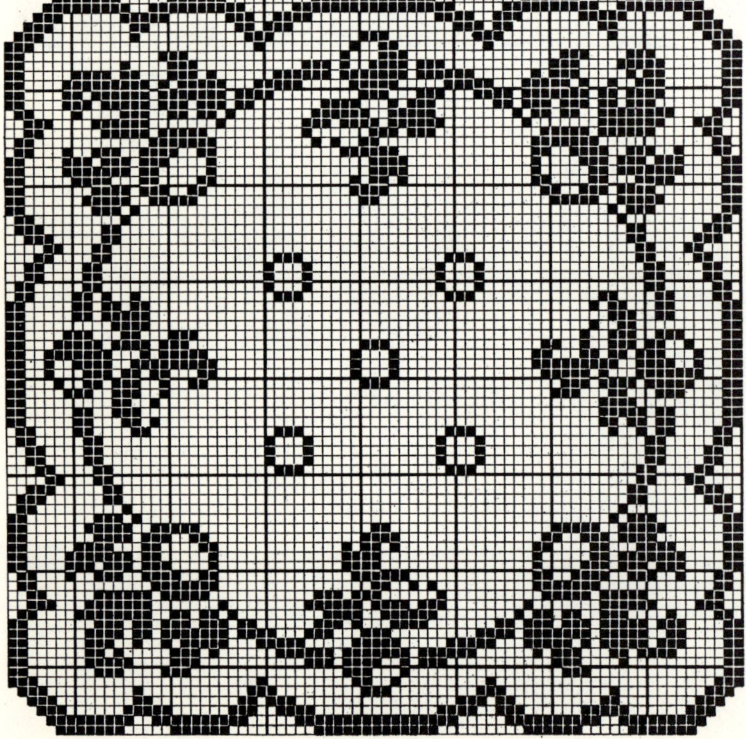

CENTERPIECE

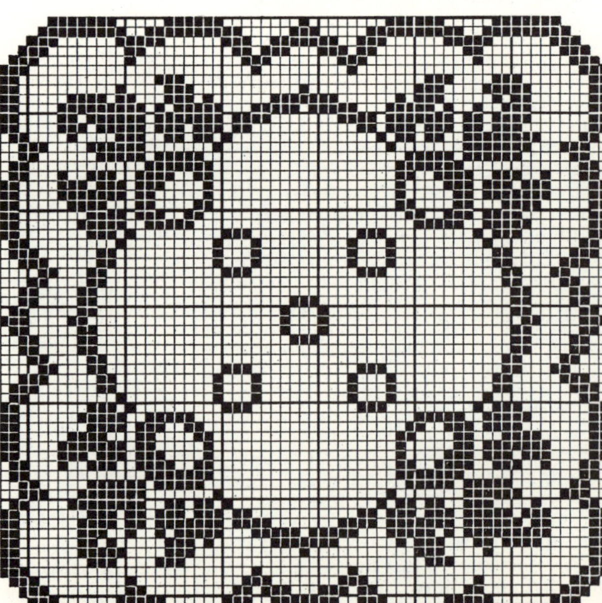

PLACE MAT

Something New!

The smartly precise outline of a square set has an elegant look when garlanded regally with roses!

Chatelaine

MATERIALS:

CLARK'S O.N.T. or J. & P. COATS BEST SIX CORD MERCERIZED CROCHET, size 30:

SMALL BALL:
CLARK'S O.N.T.—23 balls,
OR
J. & P. COATS —14 balls of White or Ecru, or 19 balls of any color.

BIG BALL:
J. & P. COATS —7 balls of White or Ecru, or 9 balls of any color.

Steel crochet hook No. 9 or 10.

This amount is sufficient for a set consisting of a centerpiece about 15½ inches square; 4 place mats about 12½ inches square; 4 bread and butter plate mats about 7½ inches square; and 4 glass mats about 5 inches square.

GAUGE: 5 sps make 1 inch; 5 rows make 1 inch.

CENTERPIECE . . . Starting at bottom of chart, ch 204. **1st row:** Dc in 4th ch from hook, dc in 20 ch (7 bls), (ch 2, skip 2 ch, dc in next ch) 5 times (5 sps); dc in 18 ch (6 bls), (ch 2, skip 2 ch, dc in next ch) 9 times; dc in 39 ch, (ch 2, skip 2 ch, dc in next ch) 9 times; dc in 18 ch, (ch 2, skip 2 ch, dc in next ch) 5 times; dc in 21 ch. Ch 5, turn. **2nd row:** Dc in 4th ch from hook, dc in next ch, dc in next 22 dc (7 bls over 7 bls), 2 dc in next sp, dc in next dc (bl over sp), (ch 2, dc in next dc) twice (2 sps over 2 sps); 10 bls, 5 sps, 17 bls, 5 sps, 10 bls, 2 sps, 7 bls, dc in next 2 dc, then make a foundation dc as follows: *Thread over, insert hook in top st of turning ch and draw a loop through; thread over and draw through 1 loop (1 ch st made, to be used as a foundation st for next dc); complete dc in usual manner.* Make 2 more foundation dc and 1 dc in the usual way (1 bl increased at both ends). Ch 5, turn. **3rd row:** Dc in 4th ch from hook, dc in next ch, 2 bls, ch 2, skip 2 dc, dc in next dc (sp over bl), 5 more sps, 5 bls, 6 sps, 3 bls, 2 sps, 4 bls, 13 sps, 4 bls, 2 sps, 3 bls, 6 sps, 5 bls, 6 sps, 1 bl, dc in next 2 dc, foundation dc in top st of turning ch, 2 more foundation dc and 1 dc in the usual way (1 bl increased at both ends). Ch 5, turn. **4th row:** 3 bls, 8 sps, 2 bls, 9 sps, 2 bls, 1 sp, 3 bls, 17 sps, 3 bls, 1 sp, 2 bls, 9 sps, 2 bls, 8 sps, 3 bls. Ch 5, turn. Starting at 5th row, follow chart until 72nd row is complete. Turn. **73rd row:** Sl st in next 3 dc, ch 3 and follow chart to within last bl (1 bl decreased at both ends). Now follow chart to complete Centerpiece. Fasten off.

PLACE MATS (Make 4) . . . Ch 162. **1st row:** 7 bls, 5 sps, 6 bls, 8 sps, 1 bl, 8 sps, 6 bls, 5 sps, 7 bls. Ch 5, turn. Follow chart to top. Fasten off.

BREAD and BUTTER PLATE MATS (Make 4) . . . Ch 102. **1st row:** (4 bls, 4 sps) twice; 1 bl, (4 sps, 4 bls) twice. Ch 5, turn. Follow chart to top. Fasten off.

GLASS MATS (Make 4) . . . Ch 60. **1st row:** 3 bls, 4 sps, 5 bls, 4 sps, 3 bls. Ch 5, turn. Follow chart to top. Fasten off.

LUNCHEON SET

ROYAL SOCIETY SIX CORD CORDICHET, Size 30:

SMALL BALL: 9 balls of any color, or LARGE BALL: 4 balls of White or Ecru.

Steel Crochet Hook No. 10.

Place Mat measures 10½ x 16 inches. Runner measures 10½ x 25 inches.

PLACE MAT (Make 2) . . . Starting lower edge, ch 182. **1st row:** Tr in 1l ch from hook, tr in next ch, (ch 3, sk 3 ch, tr in next 2 ch) 33 times; ch skip 3 ch, tr in next ch. Ch 1, tu **2nd row:** Sc in next tr, (ch 3, sc in ne 2 tr) 34 times; ch 3, skip 3 ch, sc in ne ch. Ch 7, turn. **3rd row:** Tr in ne 2 sc, (ch 3, tr in next 2 sc) 33 tim ch 3, tr in next sc. Ch 1, turn. The l 2 rows (2nd and 3rd rows) constit the pattern. Work in pattern until rows are complete.

EDGING . . . 1st rnd: Ch 1, 4 sc each sp and sc in each st around, m ing 3 sc in center st of each corner Sl st in 1st sc. **2nd rnd:** Ch 1, sc in ea sc around, making 3 sc in center sc each 3-sc group. Sl st in 1st sc. Bre off. **3rd rnd:** Attach thread in sc o 3rd tr group to left of any corn * ch 4, sc in sc over next tr group, (ch sc in same sc) 3 times; ch 4, sc in sc o next tr group, turn. D tr in 1st ch-2 ch 3, 5 d tr in same sp, (ch 3, 5 d tr next ch-2 sp) twice; ch 3, d tr in sa sp, sl st in next ch-4, ch 4, sc in sc o next tr group, turn. D tr in next d ch 5, sl st in same st, (sl st in next 3 sl st in next d tr, ch 5, holding back hook the last loop of each d tr m d tr in next 3 d tr, thread over a draw through all loops on hook—a 3 d cluster made; ch 5, sl st in next d tr times; sl st in next 3 ch, ch 5, d tr next d tr, sc in sc over next tr gro ch 4, sc in sc over next tr group. R peat from * around, making flower corner with (ch 2, sc in corner st) times (thus making 5 petals instead 3). Sl st in st where thread was attach Break off.

RUNNER . . . Ch 126. Complete as Place Mat, having 24 sps across. M 113 rows. Make Edging as for Pl Mat.

ROUND LUNCHEON SET

ROYAL SOCIETY "EVERSHEEN", 400-yard balls: 2 balls of White or Ecru.

Steel Crochet Hook No. 7.

The above amount of material is sufficient for 2 place doilies, each about 12 inches in diameter; 2 bread and butter doilies, each about 7 inches in diameter; and 2 glass doilies, each about 5 inches in diameter.

PLACE DOILY . . . Starting at center, ch 6. Join with sl st to form ring. **1st rnd:** Ch 1; 10 sc in ring. Join with sl st in 1st sc. **2nd rnd:** Ch 1, sc in same place as sl st, sc in next sc, ch 1, (sc in 2 sc, ch 1) 4 times. Join. **3rd rnd:** Ch 3, * 2 dc in next sc, ch 3, dc in next sc. Repeat from * around, ending with ch 3, sl st in 3rd st of starting chain. **4th rnd:** Ch 3, dc in same place as sl st, * dc in next dc, 2 dc in next dc, ch 4, 2 dc in next dc. Repeat from * around. Join. **5th rnd:** Ch 3, dc in same place as sl st, * dc in 3 dc, 2 dc in next dc, ch 5, 2 dc in next dc. Repeat from * around. Join. **6th rnd:** Ch 3, dc in same place as sl st, * dc in next dc, ch 5, skip 3 dc, dc in next dc, 2 dc in next dc, ch 5, 2 dc in next dc. Repeat from * around. Join. **7th rnd:** Ch 3, dc in same place as sl st, * dc in next dc, 2 dc in next dc, ch 4, 2 dc in next dc, dc in next dc, 2 dc in next dc, ch 5, 2 dc in next dc. Repeat from * around. Join. **8th rnd:** Ch 3, dc in same place as sl st, * dc in 3 dc, 2 dc in next dc, ch 4, 2 dc in next dc. Repeat from * around. Join. **9th rnd:** Ch 3, dc in same place as sl st, * dc in next dc, ch 3, skip 3 dc, dc in next dc, 2 dc in next dc, ch 4, 2 dc in next dc. Repeat from * around. Join. **10th rnd:** Ch 3, dc in same place as sl st, * dc in 2 dc, ch 3, dc in next 2 dc, 2 dc in next dc, ch 4, 2 dc in next dc. Repeat from * around. Join. **11th rnd:** Ch 3, dc in 2 dc, * 2 dc in next dc, ch 3, 2 dc in next dc, dc in 3 dc, ch 4, dc in 3 dc. Repeat from * around. Join.

12th rnd: Ch 3, dc in same place as sl st, * dc in 4 dc, ch 3, dc in 4 dc, 2 dc in next dc, ch 4, 2 dc in next dc. Repeat from * around. Join. **13th rnd:** Ch 3, dc in 4 dc, * 2 dc in next dc, ch 3, 2 dc in next dc, dc in 5 dc, ch 3, dc in 5 dc. Repeat from * around. Join. **14th rnd:** Ch 3, dc in 6 dc, * 3 dc in sp, dc in 7 dc, ch 4, dc in next 7 dc. Repeat from * around. Join. **15th rnd:** Ch 3, dc in same place as sl st, * dc in next dc, ch 5, skip 5 dc, dc in next 3 dc, ch 5, skip 5 dc, dc in next dc, 2 dc in next dc, ch 4, 2 dc in next dc. Repeat from * around. Join. **16th rnd:** Ch 3, * 2 dc in next dc, dc in next dc, ch 4, dc in next dc. Repeat from * around. Join. **17th rnd:** Ch 3, dc in same place as sl st, * dc in 3 dc, ch 4, dc in 4 dc, ch 4, dc in 3 dc, 2 dc in next dc, ch 4, 2 dc in next dc. Repeat from * around. Join. **18th rnd:** Ch 3, dc in 4 dc, * ch 4, 2 dc in next dc, dc in next 3 dc, (ch 4, dc in next 5 dc) twice. Repeat from * around. Join. **19th rnd:** Ch 3, dc in next 3 dc, * 2 dc in next dc, ch 4, dc in 5 dc, ch 4, 2 dc in next dc, dc in 4 dc, ch 4, dc in next 4 dc. Repeat from * around. Join. **20th rnd:** Ch 3, dc in 5 dc, * ch 4, dc in 4 dc, 2 dc in next dc, (ch 4, dc in 6 dc) twice. Repeat from * around. Join. **21st rnd:** Ch 3, dc in same place as sl st, * dc in 5 dc, ch 4, dc in next 6 dc, ch 4, dc in 5 dc, 2 dc in next dc, ch 4, 2 dc in next dc. Repeat from * around. Join. **22nd rnd:** Ch 3, dc in 6 dc, * ch 4, 2 dc in next dc, dc in 5 dc, (ch 4, dc in next 7 dc) twice. Repeat from * around. Join. **23rd rnd:** Ch 3, dc in 2 dc, * (2 dc in next dc, dc in 3 dc, ch 3, dc in 3 dc) twice; 2 dc in next dc, dc in 3 dc, ch 4, dc in 3 dc. Repeat from * around. Join. **24th rnd:** * Ch 5, sc in each dc to next sp, ch 5, 4 sc in sp, sc in next dc. Repeat from * around. Join and break off.

BREAD and BUTTER DOILY . . . Work same as Place Doily until 13th rnd is complete. **14th rnd:** Ch 5, * sc in each dc to next sp, ch 5, 3 sc in sp, sc in next dc. Repeat from * around. Join and break off.

GLASS DOILY . . . Work same as Place Doily until 8th rnd is complete. **9th rnd:** Ch 3, dc in same place as sl st, * dc in 5 dc, 2 dc in next dc, ch 4, 2 dc in next dc. Repeat from * around. Join. **10th rnd:** Same as 24th rnd of Place Doily. Join and break off. Starch lightly, pin out to measurement and press.

"Clover-Leaf" 5 Pc. Luncheon Set

Serve your next luncheon on hand crochet. This dainty set is ideal for a "company" luncheon and is easy to make too. It may be made into a luncheon set of any desired size.

CLOVER LEAF SQUARE

"CLOVER LEAF" 5-PIECE LUNCHEON SET

This set consists of 4 place mats, each approximately 12 inches by 18 inches and a center scarf, approximately 12 inches by 32 inches.

MATERIALS: Bucilla Wondersheen (mercerized) Cotton, Article 3666, 3 skeins,

or

Bucilla Blue Label (delustered) Cotton, Article 3457, 3 skeins.

1 Bucilla Steel Crochet Hook, Size 7, Article 4300.

Gauge: Each clover leaf square when finished should measure 2½ inches.

Filet Center—4 spaces = 1 inch, 4 rows = 1 inch.

Place Mat

FILET CENTER—Ch 42, work 1 d c in 4th st from hook, 1 d c in each of the next 2 sts on chain, * ch 2, skip 2 sts on chain, 1 d c in next st, ch 2, skip 2 sts, 1 d c in next st, ch 2, skip 2 sts, 1 d c in each of the next 4 sts; repeat from * to end of chain. **2nd row:** ch 5, turn, skip first 3 d c, work 1 d c in next st, * ch 2 and 1 d c in top of each of the next 3 d c, ch 2, skip the next 2 sts, 1 d c in next st; repeat from * across; end with ch 2, 1 s c in top st of turning chain below. **3rd row:** ch 5, turn, work 1 d c in top of 2nd d c below, ch 2 and 1 d c in top of next d c, * 2 d c in next space, 1 d c in top of next d c, ch 2 and 1 d c in top of each of the next 3 d c; repeat from * across, end with ch 2, 1 d c in 3rd st of turning chain. **4th row:** ch 5, turn, work 1 d c in top of 2nd d c below, ch 2 and 1 d c in top of next d c, * ch 2, skip 2 sts, 1 d c in top of next d c, ch 2 and 1 d c in top of each of the next 3 d c; repeat from * across, end with ch 2 and 1 d c in 3rd st of turning chain. **5th row:** ch 3, turn, work 2 d c in first space, 1 d c in top of next d c, * ch 2 and 1 d c in top of each of the next 3 d c, 2 d c in next space, 1 d c in top of next d c; repeat from * across, end with 2 d c in last space, 1 d c in 3rd st of turning chain. These last 4 rows complete the filet pattern, repeat them continuously until there are 37 rows completed from beginning, ending with the last row of pattern.

1st round of Edging: ch 1, turn, † work 1 s c in each of the first 4 d c, 3 s c in each of the next 2 spaces, 2 s c in next space, 1 s c in each of the next 4 d c, 3 s c in each of the next 2 spaces, 2 s c in next space, 1 s c in each of the next 4 d c, 3 s c in each of the next 3 spaces, 1 s c in each of the last 3 d c in row, 1 s c in top st of turning chain, working down side of strip work 3 s c under end st, * 3 s c in each of the next 3 spaces, 3 s c under end st of next row; repeat from * 8 times, then repeat from † along remaining 2 sides of strip, end with 3 s c under end st of last row, join with a slip st in first s c of round. **2nd round:** ch 9, skip 3 sts, work a treble (twice over hook) in next st, * ch 4, skip the next 4 sts, 1 treble in next st, ch 4, skip 3 sts, 1 treble in next st; repeat from * 3 times, ch 9, work a treble in same st, * ch 4, skip 4 sts, a treble in next st, ch 4, skip 4 sts, a treble in next st, ch 4, skip 5 sts, 1 treble in next st; repeat from last * to next corner, work this corner same as last, then work along remaining 2 sides of strip in same way, end with ch 4, 1 treble in joining st of round below, ch 9, join with a slip st in 5th st of chain 9 at beginning of round. **3rd round:** work 1 s c in next st, ch 1, skip next st, 1 s c in next st, * ch 1, skip 1 st, 1 s c on back thread of next treble, skip 1 st, ch 1 and 1 s c in next and every 2nd st thereafter 4 times; repeat from * 3 times, ch 1, skip next st, 1 s c on back thread of next treble, ch 1, skip 1 st, 1 s c in next st, ch 1, skip 1 st, 1 s c in next st, ch 1 and 1 s c in next (center st of chain 9) st, ch 2, 1 more s c in same st (corner), * skip 1 st, ch 1 and 1 s c in next and every 2nd st 4 times, ch 1, skip 1 st, 1 s c on back thread of next treble; repeat from last * to next corner, work this corner like last then continue to work to end of round in same way as before, end with ch 1, join with a slip st in first s c of round, slip st in next space. **4th round:** ch 1, turn, work 1 s c in first space, ch 1 and 1 s c in each space to corner, ch 1, work a group of 1 s c, ch 1, 1 s c,—all in corner space, ch 1 and 1 s c in each space to next corner, work this corner same as last, then continue around, being careful to work all corners alike, end with ch 1, join with a slip st in first s c of round, slip st in each of the next 3 sts. **5th round:** ch 9, turn, skip the first 3 spaces, 1 treble in next space, * ch 4, skip 2 spaces, 1 treble in next space; repeat from * to corner, work a group of ch 4, 1 treble, ch 9, 1 treble,—all in corner space, * ch 4, skip 1 space, a treble in next space, ch 4, skip 2 spaces, a treble in next space, ch 4, skip 2 spaces, a treble in next space, ch 4, skip 2 spaces, a treble in next space; repeat from last * to next corner, work this corner same as last, then continue to work along remaining 2 sides of strip in same way as for first 2 sides, end with ch 4, join with a slip st in 5th st of chain 9 at beginning of round and fasten off thread.

CLOVER LEAF SQUARE—Ch 3, join with a slip st into a ring; * ch 7, slip st in 4th st from hook (picot), ch 15, slip st in 12th st from hook, ch 5, turn, skip 3 sts on chain, work 1 s c in next st, ch 5, skip the next 3 sts on chain, work 1 s c in next st, ch 5, skip the next 3 sts on chain, slip st in next st (the same place as the last slip st); ch 1, turn, work 1 s c in space, 2 s d c (s d c—short d c—thread over, draw up a loop in stitch, thread over and through all 3 loops on hook) in same space, 3 d c in same space, ch 8, slip st in top of last d c made, 2 d c in same space, 2 s d c in same space, 1 s c in same space, work a group of 1 s c, 2 s d c, 3 d c, ch 8, slip st in top of last d c made, 2 more d c, 2 s d c, 1 s c,—all in each of the next 2 spaces; working along the stem, work 1 s c in each of the next 3 sts of chain, 1 s c in same place the picot was worked in, ch 3, picot, 1 s c in each of the next 3 sts on chain, slip st in ring. This completes one clover leaf pattern; repeat from * 3 times and fasten off thread. This completes one clover leaf square, make 16 of these squares.

Arrange squares around the filet center strip as shown on diagram on page 16 and tack in places as shown.

(continued on next page)

(continued)

BORDER—Working from right side, make a loop on hook and beginning in corner clover leaf on long side of mat, work a treble in corner picot, † ch 4, skip 2 sts, work a treble in next st, * ch 4, skip the next 4 sts, work a treble in next st, ch 4, work a treble in joining between picots, then ch 4, skip 2 sts on next clover leaf, 1 treble in next st; repeat from * to corner, end with ch 4, work a treble in corner picot of corner square, ch 9, 1 more treble in same place, repeat from † around entire doily, ending with ch 4 and a treble in same picot that the first treble was worked in, ch 9, join with a slip st in top of first treble of round. **2nd round:** work 1 s c in next st, ch 1, skip next st, 1 s c in next st, * ch 1, skip 1 st, 1 s c on back thread of next treble, skip 1 st, ch 1 and 1 s c in next and every 2nd st thereafter 4 times; repeat from * to center st of corner space, ch 2, 1 more s c in same st (center st of corner chain 9), skip 1 st, ch 1 and 1 s c in next and every 2nd st thereafter 4 times, ch 1, skip 1 st, 1 s c on back thread of next treble; continue to work along this side of mat in same way as first, to next corner, work this corner same as last, then continue along remaining 2 sides of mat in same way, being careful to work all corners alike, join with ch 1, slip st in first s c of round, slip st in next space. **3rd round:** ch 1, turn, work 1 s c in first space, ch 1 and 1 s c in each space to corner, ch 1, work a group of 1 s c, ch 1, 1 s c,—all in corner space, ch 1 and 1 s c in each space to next corner, work this corner same as last, then continue around being careful to work all corners alike, end with ch 1, join with a slip st in first s c of round, slip st in each of the next 3 sts. **4th round:** ch 9, turn, skip the first 3 spaces, work 1 treble in next space, † * ch 4, skip 1 space, 1 treble in next space; ch 4, skip 2 spaces, 1 treble in next space, ch 4, skip 2 spaces, a treble in next space; repeat from * 10 times, work ch 4, a group of 1 treble, ch 9, 1 more treble,—all in corner space, ch 4, skip 1 space, work a treble in next space, * ch 4, skip 2 spaces, 1 treble in next space; repeat from last * 20 times, ch 4, work a group of 1 treble, ch 9, 1 more treble,—all in corner space, ch 4, skip 2 spaces, 1 treble in next space, ch 4, skip 2 spaces, a treble in next space, then repeat from † around, end with a group of 1 treble, ch 9, 1 treble,—all in last corner space, ch 4, join with a slip st in 5th st of chain 9 at beginning of round. **Final round:** ch 1, work 1 s c in joining st below, * ch 3, picot, work 1 s c in each of the next 5 sts; repeat from * around, join with a slip st in first s c of round and fasten off thread. This completes one place-mat, make 4 of these mats.

Scarf

FILET CENTER—Follow the directions for filet center of place mat, but work until there are 93 rows completed from beginning. **Edging: ch 1,** turn, † work 1 s c in each of the first 4 d c, 3 s c in each of the next 2 spaces, 2 s c in next space, 1 s c in each of the next 4 d c, 3 s c in each of the next 2 spaces, 2 s c in next space, 1 s c in each of the next 4 d c, 3 s c in each of the next 3 spaces, 1 s c in each of the last 3 d c in row, 1 s c in top st of turning chain, working down side of strip, 3 s c under end st, * 3 s c in each of the next 3 spaces, 3 s c under end st of next row; repeat from * 22 times, then repeat from † along remaining 2 sides of strip, end with 3 s c under end st of last row, join with a slip st in first s c of round. **2nd round:** ch 9, skip 3 sts, work a treble (twice over hook) in next st, * ch 4, skip the next 4 sts, a treble in next st, ch 4, skip 3 sts, work a treble in next st; repeat from * 3 times, ch 9, work a treble in same st, * skip 4 sts, ch 4 and a treble in next and every 5th st thereafter 15 times, ch 4, skip 3 sts, a treble in next st; repeat from last * twice, then skip 4 sts, ch 4 and a treble in next and every 5th st thereafter 8 times, ch 4, skip 2 sts, work a treble in next st, work this corner same as last corner, then work along remaining 2 sides of strip in same way, end with ch 4, 1 treble in joining st of round below, ch 9, join with a slip st in 5th st of chain 9 at beginning of round. **3rd round:** same as 3rd round of edging on place-mat. **4th round:** same as 4th round of edging on place-mat. **5th round:** ch 9, turn, skip the first 3 spaces, 1 treble in next space, * ch 4, skip 2 spaces, a treble in next space; repeat from * to corner, work a group of ch 4, 1 treble, ch 9, 1 treble,—all in corner space, * ch 4, skip 1 space, work a treble in next space, ch 4, skip 2 spaces, a treble in next space, ch 4, skip 2 spaces, a treble in next space, ch 4, skip 1 space, a treble in next space, ch 4, skip 2 spaces, a treble in next space; repeat from last * to next corner, work this corner same as last, then continue to work along remaining 2 sides of strip in same way as for first 2 sides, end with ch 4, join with a slip st in 5th st of chain 9 at beginning of round and fasten off thread.

CLOVER LEAF SQUARE—Following the directions for clover leaf square on place mat, make 28 of these squares.

Arrange squares around center of scarf and tack in places in same way as for place-mat as shown on diagram, having 12 squares in length and 4 squares in width.

BORDER—Follow the directions for first 3 rounds of border of place mat. **4th round:** ch 9, turn, skip the first 3 spaces, work 1 treble in next space, † * ch 4, skip 1 space, 1 treble in next space, ch 4, skip 2 spaces, 1 treble in next space, ch 4, skip 2 spaces, a treble in next space; repeat from * 21 times, ch 4, skip next space, a treble in next space, work ch 4, a group of 1 treble, ch 9, 1 more treble,—all in corner space, ch 4, skip 1 space, work a treble in next space, * ch 4, skip 2 spaces, 1 treble in next space; repeat from last * 20 times, ch 4, work a group of 1 treble, ch 9, 1 more treble,—all in corner space, ch 4, skip 2 spaces, 1 treble in next space, ch 4, skip 2 spaces, a treble in next space, then repeat from † around, end with a group of 1 treble, ch 9, 1 treble,—all in last corner space, ch 4, join with a slip st in 5th st of chain 9 at beginning of round. **Final round:** ch 1, work 1 s c in joining st below, * ch 3, picot, work 1 s c in each of the next 5 sts; repeat from * around, join with a slip st in first s c of round and fasten off thread.

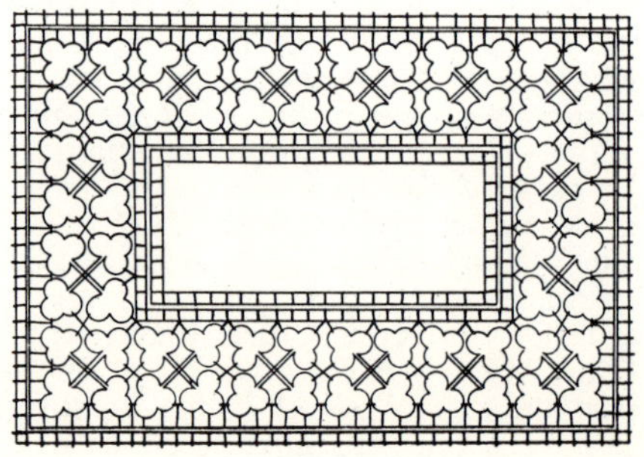

SNOWDRIFT

Tiny medallions of jewel-like beauty form interesting hexagon doilies.

MATERIALS: For best results use—

CLARK'S O.N.T. OR J. & P. COATS
BEST SIX CORD MERCERIZED CROCHET, Size 50:

SMALL BALL:

CLARK'S O.N.T.—*14 balls of White or Ecru, or 19 balls of any color.*
OR
J. & P. COATS—*10 balls of White or Ecru, or 14 balls of any color.*

BIG BALL:

CLARK'S O.N.T. OR J. & P. COATS—*6 balls of White or Ecru.*

MILWARD'S *steel crochet hook No. 12 or 13.*

Completed runner measures about 13½ x 31½ inches; each place mat measures about 12¼ x 12¼ inches across center.

GAUGE: Each motif measures 1¾ inches in diameter.

PLACE MATS *(Make 6)* ... First Motif... Ch 10, join with sl st. **1st rnd:** Ch 3, 23 d c in ring. Join to 3rd st of ch-3. **2nd rnd:** Ch 4, * d c in next d c, ch 1. Repeat from * around. Join last ch-1 to 1st sp. **3rd rnd:** Ch 10, * skip 1 sp, tr in next sp, ch 6. Repeat from * around. Join last ch-6 to 4th st of ch-10. **4th rnd:** * Ch 2, skip 2 ch, d c in next ch, ch 2, d c in next ch, ch 2, s c in next tr. Repeat from * around; join. **5th rnd:** * Ch 2, d c in next d c, ch 2, d c in ch-2 sp, ch 2, d c in next d c, ch 2, s c in next s c. Repeat from * around. Fasten off.

Second Motif... Work 4 rnds as for 1st motif. **5th rnd:** Ch 2, d c in next d c, * ch 1, sl st in corresponding sp on 1st motif, ch 1, d c in next sp on second motif, ch 1, sl st in next sp on first motif, ch 1, d c in next d c on second motif, ch 2, s c in next s c, ch 2, d c in next d c. Repeat from * once more; complete rnd as for 1st motif.

Make 2 more motifs, joining as 2nd was joined to 1st. This completes one strip. Make another strip of 5 motifs, joining 2 points of each motif to 2 points of adjacent motifs as before (motifs fall between those of previous strip). Continue thus, making 1 strip of 6 motifs, 1 strip of 7 motifs, then 1 strip of 6 motifs, 1 strip of 5 motifs, and 1 strip of 4 motifs. This completes 1 place mat.

RUNNER... Make 1st strip of 14 motifs, then 1 strip of 15 motifs, 1 strip of 16 motifs, 1 strip of 17 motifs, 1 strip of 18 motifs, 1 strip of 17 motifs, 1 strip of 16 motifs, 1 strip of 15 motifs, and last strip of 14 motifs.

Tulip Luncheon Set

MATERIALS: *7 balls Cynthia Mercerized Crochet Cotton, size 20, White or Ecru.*

Boye Steel Crochet Hook No. 7 or 8.

Buy Sufficient Thread at one time.

This material is sufficient for 4 place mats, each about 11 x 17½ inches (6 squares joined together), and a center mat about 16½ x 26½ inches (15 squares).

Each square is composed of 4 tulips and should measure about 5½ inches across.

FIRST TULIP OF FIRST SQUARE— **Row 1:** Ch 20, 1 D C in the 4th ch from hook, 1 D C in each of the next 15 chs, 2 D C in the last ch, ch 2, 2 D C in the same ch, 1 D C in each st on other side of foundation ch (17 sts), ch 1, turn. **Row 2:** Slip st in each of first 3 D C, ch 3, 1 D C in each D C, 2 D C in space made by ch-2, ch 2, 2 D C in same space, 1 D C in each D C on other side of tulip to within 2 sts of end, ch 1, turn (19 D C on each side counting 1st ch-3). **Rows 3-4-5-6:** Repeat row 2. **Row 7:** Ch 5, 1 S C in last st of row 5, * ch 5, 1 S C in next point, repeat from * 3 times, ch 5, 1 S C in foundation ch, ch 5, 1 S C in first point on other side, * ch 5, 1 S C in next point, repeat from * to last point (12 ch-5 loops), ch 5, 1 S C in 4th D C, * ch 5, skip 2 D C, 1 S C in next D C, repeat from * 4 times, ch 11, 1 S C in 1st D C on other side, * ch 5, skip 2 D C, 1 S C in next D C, repeat from * 5 times, join with slip st in 1st ch of 1st ch-5 loop. Fasten off.

SECOND TULIP OF FIRST SQUARE: Repeat **Rows 1-6** inclusive. **Row 7:** * Ch 5, 1 S C in last st of row 5, repeat from * around top of tulip to last point on other side, join to first tulip as follows: ch 2, slip st in 3rd ch of last ch-5 loop on first tulip, ch 2, skip 2 D C on second tulip, 1 S C in next D C, * ch 2, slip st in 3rd ch of next ch-5 loop on first tulip, ch 2, skip 2 D C, 1 S C in next D C, repeat from * 4 times, ch 5, join with slip st in 6th ch of ch-11 on first tulip, ch 5, 1 S C in first D C on other side, * ch 5, skip 2 D C, 1 S C in next D C, repeat from * 5 times, join with slip st in first ch of 1st ch-5 loop.

THIRD TULIP OF FIRST SQUARE: Work the same as second tulip, joining to second tulip in same manner as the second tulip was joined to first and to the first tulip with ch 5 and slip st in 6th ch of ch-11 on first tulip.

FOURTH TULIP OF FIRST SQUARE: Work the same as third tulip, joining to third and first tulips in the same way. This completes the first square.

FIRST TULIP OF SECOND SQUARE: Repeat **Rows 1-6** inclusive. **Row 7:** Ch 2, join to fourth tulip with slip st in center ch of ch-5 loop on last point, ch 2, 1 S C in next point, * ch 2, slip st in 3rd ch of next ch-5 loop on fourth tulip, ch 2, 1 S C in next point, repeat from * 4 times, * ch 5, 1 S C in 1st point on other side, repeat from * to last point, * ch 5, skip 2 D C, 1 S C in next D C, repeat from * 5 times, ch 11, 1 S C in first D C on other side, * ch 5, skip 2 D C, 1 S C in next D C, repeat from * 5 times, join with slip st in 1st ch of ch-2 at beginning of row. Fasten off.

SECOND TULIP OF SECOND SQUARE: Work the same as other tulips to **6th row** inclusive. **7th row:** Work 6 ch-5 loops on first side of tulip, ch 2, join with slip st in 1st ch-5 loop on adjacent side of 3rd tulip of first square, ch 2, 1 S C in 1st point on other side, ch 2, * slip st in next ch-5 loop on 3rd tulip, ch 2, 1 S C in next point, repeat from * to last point, then join to 1st tulip of second square in same manner, with ch 5 at base of tulip, join with slip st in 6th ch of ch-11 on 1st tulip, ch 5, 1 S C in 1st D C on other side, * ch 5, skip 2 D C, 1 S C in next D C, repeat from * 5 times, join with slip st in 1st ch of 1st ch-5 loop. Fasten off.

Work **third and fourth tulips**, joining to first and second tulips, in same manner.

Work the **third square**, joining to 3rd and 4th tulips of second square. This completes the first section of place mat.

Work the **second section** alongside of first section, joining adjacent tulips as before.

FILL-IN MOTIF: Attach thread in corner point of tulip, ch 9, join with slip st in corner point on opposite tulip, slip st over ch-2 joining between squares, slip st in joining slip st, ch 4, slip st in 5th ch of ch-9, ch 4, slip st in slip st joining opposite two tulips, slip st over ch to corner point, ch 4, slip st in 5th ch of ch-9, ch 4, slip st in opposite point. Fasten off.

EDGING: Attach thread in a space on edge. 3 S C in space, ch 3, join with slip st in 1st st of ch-3 (picot), 3 S C in same space, * 3 S C in next space, ch-3 picot, 3 S C in same space, repeat from * around entire mat, join and fasten off.

CENTER MAT: Work 5 sections of 3 squares each, joining in same manner.

Blue Ribbon Luncheon Set

National Crochet Contest
Prize Winning Design

Materials: Clark's O.N.T. "Brilliant," 67 balls of Yellow and 15 balls of Nile Green.
Milward's steel crochet hook No. 12.

This material is sufficient for 4 place mats, each about 11 x 16 inches, and a center mat about 16 x 36 inches. Each motif measures about 1 inch square.

Place Mat. Starting at long side, make a strip of 16 motifs, as follows:

First Motif. Starting at center, with Yellow ch 8. Join with sl st to form ring. **1st rnd:** Ch 3, 19 d c in ring. Join with sl st between ch-3 and 1st d c. **2nd rnd:** Ch 5 (to count as d c and ch-2), * d c between next 2 d c, ch 2. Repeat from * around, ending rnd with sl st in first ch-2 sp (20 sps). **3rd rnd:** Ch 3, 2 d c in same sp as sl st, 3 d c in each of next 3 sps, * ch 8, skip 1 sp, 3 d c in each of next 4 sps. Repeat from * 2 more times, ch 8, join with sl st to 3rd st of ch-3 first made. Break off. This completes first motif.

Second Motif. Work as for first motif to 2nd rnd incl. **3rd rnd:** Ch 3, 2 d c in same sp as sl st, join with s c between 3rd and 4th d c on one side of first motif (always keeping right side of work on top), make 3 d c in next sp back on second motif, s c between 6th and 7th d c of same side of first motif, 3 d c in next sp back on second motif, s c between 9th and 10th d c of same side of first motif, 3 d c in next sp back on second motif, ch 4, join with sl st to ch-8 loop of first motif, ch 4, skip 1 sp on second motif, 3 d c in next sp. Complete this rnd as in first motif, with no more joinings to within the last ch-8. Then ch 4, join with sl st to ch-8 on first motif, ch 4, join with sl st to 3rd st of ch-3 first made on second motif. Break off.

Make another motif of Nile Green, 10 of Yellow, 1 of Nile Green and 2 of Yellow, joining each motif to previous one as second was joined to first (this completes a strip of 16 motifs).

Hereafter follow diagram, making 9 more strips of 16 motifs and joining as follows: Work first motif of second strip and join to lower edge of first strip.

Second Motif. Work as before to 2nd rnd incl. **3rd rnd:** Ch 3, 2 d c in same sp as sl st, 3 d c in each of next 3 sps, ch 4, sl st in ch-8 loop of first motif of second strip, ch 4, skip 1 sp on second motif, 3 d c in next sp, s c between 3rd and 4th d c of first motif, 3 d c back in next sp of second motif, s c between 6th and 7th d c of first motif, 3 d c back in next sp of second motif, s c between 9th and 10th d c of first motif, 3 d c back in next sp of second motif, ch 4, sl st in ch-8 loop of corner, ch 4, skip 1 sp, 3 d c in next sp and continue to join next side of motif to adjacent side of second motif of first strip, as before, and complete rnd. Continue in this manner until place mat is complete. Make 3 more place mats same as this.

Center Mat. Work exactly as for place mat. Then make 16 more strips with Yellow only, and join as before. Work to correspond with opposite end.

Homespun Luncheon Set

Can't you picture gay flowered pottery on this colorful luncheon set? Ever so easy to make — and the three toned embroidery adds the smart peasant touch.

Materials: J. & P. Coats Knit-Cro-Sheen, 13 balls of Dk. Ecru, and 1 ball each of Skipper Blue, Hunter's Green and Spanish Red.

Milward's steel crochet hook No. 5.

This material is sufficient for 4 place mats, each about 11 x 16 inches, and a center mat about 14 x 36 inches.

Center Mat. Starting at short side, with Dk. Ecru make a chain to measure about 20 inches, turn. **1st row:** S c in 3rd ch from hook, * ch 1, skip 1 ch, s c in next ch. Repeat from * across until row measures 14 inches. Cut off remaining chain. Ch 2, turn. **2nd row:** S c in 1st s c, * ch 1, skip ch-1, s c in next s c. Repeat from * across. Ch 2, turn. Repeat the last row until piece measures 36 inches. Break off. Attach Skipper Blue and make a row of s c, with ch-1 between each s c, all around edges; at corners, make 2 s c with ch-1 between.

Fringe. Cut 3 strands, each 3 inches long, of Dk. Ecru. Double these strands, forming a loop. Pull loop through ch-1 sp, and draw loose ends of fringe through this loop. Pull tight. Knot a fringe in each ch-1 sp all around. Trim evenly.

Embroidery. With Hunter's Green, make a double block of cross stitch in each corner, starting 1 inch in from edge and making a cross st over each s c. Then, with Skipper Blue, starting at center of double block, work a row of cross stitch across one side to center of double block at opposite side. Then, at center of this row, work a triangle, having lower point toward center of runner. Work other sides to correspond. Now, with Spanish Red, work a row of cross stitch on both sides of Skipper Blue, starting at corner of one block and working across to corresponding corner of block at opposite side. Work other sides to correspond.

Place Mats (Make 4). Starting at long side, make a chain to measure about 20 inches. Work exactly as for center mat until row measures 16 inches. Cut off remaining chain. Then work as for center mat until piece measures 11 inches. Break off. Complete place mat as for center mat.

SQUARE TABLE MAT

Materials: 1 Ball CYNTHIA Mercerized Crochet Cotton, White or Ecru Size 30. Boye Steel Crochet Hook, No. 9 or 10.
When completed mat measures 12 x 14 inches.
Gauge: 2 sps make 1 inch; 5 rows make 1 inch.

Beginning at lower edge, ch 170, turn.
1st row: D C in 14th ch from hook, * ch 5, skip 5 ch, D C in next ch (1 space), repeat from * across (27 spaces), ch 6, turn.
2nd row: S C over ch 5, ch 3, D C in D C (a V at beginning of row), ch 3, S C over next ch 5, ch 3, D C in next D C (a V), work another V over next ch 5, 3 D C in next sp, ch 2, D C in next D C, a V over next ch 5, ch 2, 3 D C over next ch 5, D C in next D C, a V over each of next 15 ch 5 spaces, 3 D C, ch 2 over next ch 5, D C in next D C, a V over next ch 5, ch 2, 3 D C over next ch 5, D C in next D C, a V over each of last 3 ch 5 spaces, ending with D C in 3rd st of turning ch, ch 8, turn.
3rd row: D C in D C, ch 5 space over each of next 2 Vs, D C in each of next 4 D C, 2 D C over ch 2 space, D C in next D C, ch 5 sp over next V, 2 D C over next ch 2 space, D C in each of next 4 D C, ch 5 space over each of next 15 Vs, D C in each of next 4 D C, 2 D C over ch 2 space, D C in next D C, ch 5 space over next V, 2 D C over next ch 2 space, D C in each of next 4 D C, ch 5 space over each of last 3 Vs, ending with D C in 3rd ch of turning ch 6, ch 6, turn.
Continue in this manner, alternating the rows of Vs and spaces, and following chart for pattern.

EDGING

1st row: Starting on lower edge in corner ch st, ch 3, 2 D C in same st as ch 3, ch 2, 3 more D C in same st, * ch 5, skip 1 D C, 3 D C in next D C, ch 2, 3 more D C in same st, repeat from * to next corner (14 shells), ch 5, work a shell in corner st, ch 5, skip 3 spaces on side edge, a shell in next space, * ch 5, skip 4 spaces, a shell in next space, repeat from * to next corner, skipping only 2 spaces before corner shell, continue around top edge and other side in same way, joining with slip st in 3rd st of beginning ch 3.
2nd row: Slip st over to corner space, ch 3, 2 D C in same space, ch 2, 3 D C in same space, ch 5, * 3 D C in next ch 2 space, ch 2, 3 more D C in same space, ch 5, repeat from * around, join with slip st in 3rd st of ch 3.
3rd row: Slip st over to corner space, ch 6, slip st in 3rd ch from hook (picot), * D C in same space, ch 3, slip st in 1st st of ch (picot) repeat from * 3 times, work 1 more D C in same space, ch 3, 1 S C over ch 5 of 1st and 2nd rows (catching both chs together), ch 3, continue around entire mat, working a shell with picot between D Cs in each space, and 1 S C over ch 5 between shells, join with slip st in 3rd ch of beginning ch 6 and fasten off.

Hostess

MATERIALS REQUIRED

American Thread Company "Star" or "Gem" Mercerized Crochet Cotton Size 20

"Star" Mercerized Crochet Cotton, Small Ball,
White or Ecru, 10 Balls. Colors 13 balls.
"Star" Mercerized Crochet Cotton, Large Ball,
White or Ecru, 5 Balls.
Dk. Cream or Dk. Linen, 6 Balls.
"Gem" Mercerized Crochet Cotton,
White, Ecru or Dk. Ecru, 4 Balls.
Steel Crochet Hook #12 or #13.
1 yd.—36 inch linen.

PLATE DOILY. Ch 155 for 50 open meshes, work 1st d c in 8th ch for hook, * ch 2, skip 2 sts, d c in next st, repeat from * to end of row, ch 5, turn and work back and forth according to diagram. Finish with a row of s c.

CENTER DOILY. Ch 353 for 116 open meshes, work one row of open meshes.

2nd to 34th rows work 33 open meshes, next 50 meshes follow chart and work 33 open meshes.

On each end 34 meshes, follow chart up and down beginning with the 2nd row. Ch 144 for center 48 meshes and work basket design working back and forth according to diagram. Finish with a row of s c. Work a row of s c around linen center and sew to filet crochet. Finish edges of linen section of plate doilies with a row of s c, sew filet motif in position and finish luncheon set with the following edge.

Join thread in corner and work 1 s c, ch 3, skip 1 s c, * work 3 d c cluster in next st, ch 4, sl st in cluster for picot, ch 3, skip 3 sts, s c in next st, ch 3, skip 3 sts, repeat from * all around skipping only 1 s c at corners.

Passion Flower Luncheon Set

This mat may be made with any of the American Thread Company products listed below:

Material	Quantity	Size of Needle	Approx. Size of Mat
"STAR" Crochet Cotton Article 20, Size 30	4 Balls White, 5 Balls Shaded Lavenders 1 Ball each Yellow and Green	11 or 12	12x17 inches
or			
"STAR" Crochet Cotton Article 30, Size 30	14 Balls White, 13 Balls Shaded Lavenders 2 Balls Green, 1 Ball Yellow	11 or 12	12x17 inches
or			
"GEM" Crochet Cotton Article 35, Size 30	3 Balls White, 4 Balls Shaded Lavenders 1 Ball each Green and Yellow	11 or 12	12x17 inches
or			
"SILLATEEN SANSIL" Article 102	14 Balls White, 13 Balls Shaded Lavenders 2 Balls Green, 1 Ball Yellow	10	13x18 inches

Will make 4 mats. Plain Color may be used if desired.

Ch 6, join to form a ring, ch 5, d c in ring, * ch 2, d c in ring, repeat from * 5 times, ch 2, join in 3rd st of ch.
2nd Row—Sl st into loop, ch 3 (always counts as ⅓ part of 1st cluster st) and work a cluster st in each loop with ch 5 between cluster sts, (cluster st: thread over needle, insert in space, pull through, thread over and work off 2 loops, * thread over needle, insert in same space, pull through, thread over and work off 2 loops, repeat from * once, thread over and pull through all loops at one time) ch 5, join in top of 1st cluster st.
3rd Row—Sl st into loop, ch 3, cluster st in same space, ch 4, cluster st in same space, * ch 4, 2 cluster sts with ch 4 between in next loop, repeat from * all around, ch 4, join.
4th Row—Sl st into loop, * ch 6, s c in next loop, repeat from * all around ending row with ch 2, tr c in sl st, this brings thread in position for next row.
5th Row—Ch 3, cluster st in same space, ch 5, cluster st in same space, * ch 5, s c in next loop, ch 5, sl st in next loop, ch 3, sl st in same loop, ch 5, s c in next loop, ch 5, 1 cluster st, ch 5, 1 cluster st in next loop (corner), repeat from * twice, ch 5, s c in next loop, ch 5, sl st in next loop, ch 3, sl st in same space, ch 5, s c in next loop, ch 5, join.
6th Row—Sl st into loop, ch 3 and work 2 cluster sts with ch 5 between in same space, * ch 5, s c in next ch 5 loop, repeat from * 3 times, ch 5, 2 cluster sts with ch 5 between in next loop, repeat from 1st * twice, * ch 5, s c in next ch 5 loop, repeat from * 3 times, ch 5, join.
7th Row—Sl st into loop, ch 3, 2 cluster sts with ch 5 between in same space, * ch 7, 2 cluster sts with ch 5 between in same space, ch 5, skip 1 loop, s c in next loop, ch 5, cluster st in next loop, ch 5, s c in next loop, ch 5, skip 1 loop, 2 cluster sts with ch 5 between in next loop, repeat from * all around ending row to correspond, join, break thread. Work a 2nd motif joining it to 1st motif in last row as follows, sl st into loop, ch 3, cluster st **in**

same space, ch 5, cluster st in same space, ch 3, s c in corner loop of 1st motif, ch 3, cluster st in same space of 2nd motif, ch 2, s c in next loop of 1st motif, ch 2, cluster st in same space of 2nd motif, ch 2, s c in next loop of 1st motif, ch 2, skip 1 loop of 2nd motif, s c in next loop, ch 2, s c in next loop of 1st motif, ch 2, cluster st in next loop of 2nd motif, ch 2, s c in next loop of 1st motif, ch 2, s c in next loop of 2nd motif, ch 2, s c in next loop of 1st motif, ch 2, skip 1 loop of 2nd motif, cluster st in next loop, ch 2, s c in next loop of 1st motif, ch 2, cluster st in same space of 2nd motif, ch 3, s c in corner loop of 1st motif, ch 3, cluster st in same space of 2nd motif, ch 5, cluster st in same space and finish row same as 1st motif. Join all motifs in same manner having 3 motifs in width and 5 motifs in length.

Join 1 motif at each corner, joining in corner loop only. (19 motifs for each mat). With White work a row of s c all around working 4 s c over each loop and 1 s c in each cluster st and each s c working 3 s c in loop before joining of motifs, 1 s c in joining, 3 s c in next loop of next motif and 7 s c in corner loops of the single motifs, break thread.

FLOWERS—With Green ch 10, join to form a ring, ch 1 and work 20 s c in ring, join.

2nd Row—Ch 4, 1 d c in next s c, * ch 1, d c in next s c, repeat from * all around, ch 1, join in 3rd st of ch (20 d c), break Green.

3rd Row—Attach Shaded Lavenders, ch 1 and work 2 s c in each mesh, join (40 s c).

Next Row—Start Petal: * 1 s c in each of the next 5 s c, ch 1, turn.

Next Row—2 s c in 1st s c, 1 s c in each of the next 3 s c, 2 s c in next s c (7 s c), ch 1, turn. Working in s c, work 5 rows even, then decrease 1 st at beginning of each row until 1 st remains, (to decrease; insert needle in next st, pull loop through, insert needle in next st, pull loop through, thread over and pull through all loops at one time) ch 1, sl st down side of petal, repeat from * all around (8 petals), break thread. Work a 2nd flower joining 1st 2 petals to tip of 1st 2 petals of 1st flower with a sl st, complete next 6 petals without joining. Join all flowers in same manner leaving 2 petals free at top and lower edge of each flower. Three flowers are used on each short side and 5 flowers on each long side.

Stamens * With Green ch 16, insert needle in 2nd st from hook and pull loop through, insert needle in each of the next 4 sts of ch pulling a loop through each st, thread over and pull through all 6 loops on needle at one time, sl st in each remaining st of ch, repeat from * once, break thread leaving an end to sew. With Yellow, work 2 more stamens in same manner. Pull through center of flower. Sew firmly on wrong side of flower. Finish each flower in same manner. Working across long side attach Green in center st of 2nd free corner of single motif, ch 3, sl st in same space for picot, 1 s c in each of the next 4 s c, ch 3, sl st in top of last s c for picot, * 1 s c in each of the next 5 s c, ch 3, sl st in top of last s c for picot, repeat from * 5 times, 1 s c in each of the next 4 s c, picot, 1 s c in each of the next 4 s c, holding the wrong side of 5 flower strip toward you, ch 7, sl st in 4th row from tip on left hand side of petal of 2nd free petal from joining (about ¼ inch from tip of petal), ch 1, turn, s c in 2nd ch from hook, 1 s c in each of the next 5 sts of ch, sl st in top of last s c made on motif, ch 7, sl st ¼ inch from tip on right hand side of next petal, ch 1, turn, s c in 2nd ch from hook, 1 s c in each of the next 5 sts of ch, sl st in top of last s c made on motif, 1 s c in each of the next 5 s c, picot, 1 s c in each of the next 5 s c, ch 1, sl st in tip of same petal of flower, ch 1, sl st in top of last s c made on motif, 1 s c in each of the next 5 s c, ch 3, sl st on left hand side of same petal about ¼ inch from tip of same petal, ch 3, sl st in top of last s c made on motif, ch 3, sl st on right hand side of next petal (when working on side of petals always sl st about same distance from tip of each petal), ch 3, sl st in top of last s c made on motif, 1 s c in each of the next 5 s c, ch 1, sl st in tip of same petal, ch 1, sl st in top of last s c made on motif, 1 s c in each of the next 5 s c, picot, 1 s c in each of the next 5 s c, ch 7, sl st on left hand side of same petal, ch 1, turn and work back on ch same as before, sl st in top of last s c made on motif, 1 s c in each of the next 4 s c, picot, 1 s c in each of the next 4 s c on next motif, ch 7, sl st on right side of next petal of same flower, ch 1, turn and work back on ch same as before, sl st in top of last s c made on motif, 1 s c in each of the next 5 s c, picot, 1 s c in each of the next 5 s c, * ch 1, sl st in tip of same petal, ch 1, turn, sl st in top of last s c made on motif, 1 s c in each of the next 5 s c, ch 3, sl st on left hand side of same petal, ch 3, turn, sl st in top of last s c made on motif, ch 3, sl st on right hand side of next petal, ch 3, turn, sl st in top of last s c made on motif, 1 s c in each of the next 5 s c, ch 1, sl st in tip of same petal, ch 1, turn, sl st in top of last s c made on motif, 1 s c in each of the next 5 s c, picot, 1 s c in each of the next 5 s c, ch 7, sl st on left hand side of same petal, ch 1, turn and work back on ch same as before, sl st in top of last s c made on motif, 1 s c in each of the next 3 s c, ch 9, sl st in next petal of same flower to right of joining, ch 1, turn, s c in 2nd ch from hook, 1 s c in each of the next 7 sts of ch, sl st in top of last s c made on motif, s c in next s c, ch 9, sl st in corresponding petal of next flower to left of joining, ch 1, turn and work back on ch same as before, sl st in top of last s c made on motif, 1 s c in each of the next 4 s c of next motif, ch 7, sl st on right hand side of next petal of same flower, ch 1, turn and work back on ch same as before, sl st in top of last s c made on motif, 1 s c in each of the next 5 s c, picot, 1 s c in each of the next 5 s c, repeat from * 3 times, ch 1, sl st in tip of same petal, ch 1, sl st in top of last s c made on motif, 1 s c in each of the next 5 s c, ch 3, sl st on left hand side of same petal, ch 3, sl st in top of last s c made on motif, ch 3, sl st on right hand side of next petal of same flower, ch 3, turn, sl st in top of last s c made on motif, 1 s c in each of the next 5 s c, ch 1, sl st in tip of same petal of flower, ch 1, turn, sl st in top of last s c made on motif, 1 s c in each of the next 5 s c, picot, 1 s c in each of the next 5 s c, ch 7, sl st on left hand side of same petal, ch 1, turn and work back on ch same as before, sl st in top of last s c made on motif, 1 s c in each of the next 4 s c, picot, 1 s c in each of the next 4 s c of single motif, ch 7, sl st on right hand side of next petal, ch 1, turn and work down on ch same as before, sl st in top of last s c made on motif, 1 s c in each of the next 5 s c, picot, 1 s c in each of the next 5 s c, ch 1, sl st in tip of same petal, ch 1, turn, sl st in top of last s c on motif, 1 s c in each of the next 5 s c, ch 3, sl st on side of same petal, ch 3, sl st in top of last s c made on motif, ch 3, sl st on side of next petal, ch 3, sl st in top of last s c made on motif, 1 s c in each of the next 5 s c, ch 1, sl st in tip of same petal, ch 1, turn, sl st in top of last s c made on motif, 1 s c in each of the next 5 s c, picot, 1 s c in each of the next 5 s c, ch 7, sl st on left hand side of same petal, ch 1, turn and work down on ch same as before, sl st in top of last s c made on motif, ch 7, sl st on right hand side of next petal, ch 1, turn and work down on ch same as before, sl st in top of last s c made on motif, then work 1 s c in each s c on the next 2 sides of single motif, working a picot on top of every 5th st having the picots over the cluster sts of previous row and 1 picot in center st at corners. Join next 3 flowers across short side in same manner and finish other long and short side to correspond.

STAR FILET LUNCHEON SET

Materials: 6 Balls CYNTHIA Mercerized Crochet Cotton, Size 20, White or Ecru. Boye Steel Crochet Hook, No. 8.

Gauge: 4 sps make 1 inch; 5 rows make 1 inch.

The runner and place mats are made of individual motifs which are sewed together. When completed the runner measures 16½ x 24½ inches and each place mat 10½ x 18½ inches.

MOTIF

Ch 85. 1 D C in 7th ch from hook, * ch 2, skip 2 ch, 1 D C in next ch, repeat from * 25 times (27 sps). Ch 5, turn.

2nd row: * 1 D C in next D C, ch 2, repeat from * 26 times, 1 D C in 3rd st of turning ch. Ch 5, turn.

3rd row: 1 D C in next D C, ch 2, 1 D C in next D C, 2 D C in next sp, 1 D C in next D C, 2 D C in next sp, 1 D C in next D C (2 blocks), ch 2, 1 D C in next D C, 2 D C in next sp, 1 D C in next D C (1 block), * ch 2, 1 D C in next D C, repeat from * twice (3 sps), 2 D C in next sp, 1 D C in next D C, * ch 2, 1 D C in next D C, repeat from * 6 times, 2 D C in next sp, 1 D C in next D C, * ch 2, 1 D C in next D C, repeat from * twice, 2 D C in next sp, 1 D C in next D C, ch 2, 1 D C in next D C, 2 D C in next sp, 1 D C in next D C, 2 D C in next sp, 1 D C in next D C, ch 2, 1 D C in next D C, ch 2, 1 D C in 3rd st of ch 5. Ch 5, turn.

Work in same manner, following chart until motif is completed. Make 6 motifs for each place mat and 12 motifs for the runner, joining as follows: using same thread as for crocheting, sew motifs together with over and over stitch, sewing through back threads of edge stitches. When motifs are joined work edging around each place mat and runner.

EDGE

1 S C in corner sp, ch 3, * 1 Tr, 2 D Tr (double treble), 1 Tr in next sp (a shell), ch 3, skip 1 sp, 1 S C in next sp, ch 3, skip 1 sp, repeat from * around entire edge, working 1 S C in the joining between squares and a shell in each sp immediately before and after each corner sp, join with slip st in 1st S C and fasten off.

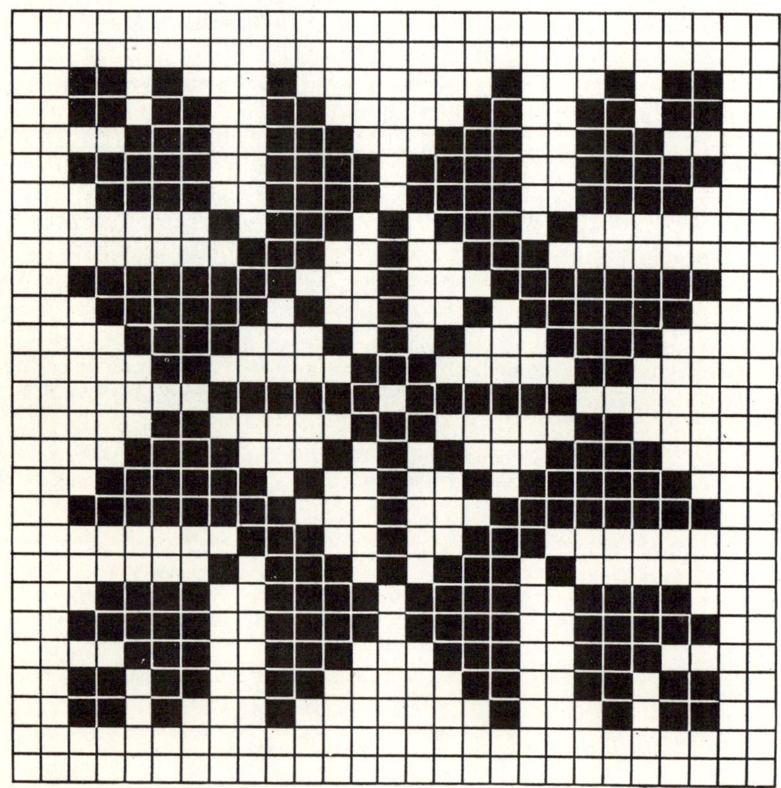

Use the Star Filet motif for a tablecloth. 132 motifs will complete a tablecloth 56 x 72 inches and requires only 22 balls of Cynthia Mercerized Crochet Cotton, size 20.

STAR FILET LUNCHEON SET

"Rose Filet" 5-Piece Luncheon Set

A very charming set for Luncheon or Supper Service. It is easily made in simple Filet stitch edged with a smart cluny scallop.

"Rose Filet" 5-Piece Luncheon Set

This set consists of 4 place mats, each approximately 12 inches by 18 inches and a scarf, approximately 12 inches by 32 inches.

MATERIALS: Bucilla Wondersheen (mercerized) Cotton, Article 3666, 3 skeins,

or

Bucilla Blue Label (delustered) Cotton, Article 3457, 3 skeins.

1 Bucilla Steel Crochet Hook, Size 9, Article 4300.

Gauge: 4 spaces = 1 inch 4 rows = 1 inch

PLACE MAT—Ch 117, work 1 d c in 9th st from hook, * ch 2, skip 2 sts on chain, 1 d c in next st; repeat from * to end of chain (37 spaces in row). **2nd row:** ch 5, turn, 1 d c in top of 2nd d c below, ch 2 and 1 d c in top of each d c across, ch 2, work 1 d c in 6th st of turning chain below. **3rd row (see chart):** ch 5, turn, work 1 d c in 2nd d c of row below, ch 2 and 1 d c in top of each of the next 2 d c, 2 d c in next space, 1 d c in top of next d c (a solid block), 2 d c in next space, 1 d c in top of next d c, ch 2 and 1 d c in top of each of the next 4 d c below, work a group of 7 d c over the next 2 spaces, continue in this way to follow chart to end of row. **4th row (see chart):** ch 5, turn, work 1 d c in top of 2nd d c below, ch 2 and 1 d c in top of next d c, work a solid block in next space, 2 spaces over the 2 solid blocks below, 1 solid block over next space, 2 spaces over the next 2 spaces, a solid block over next space, continue in this way to follow chart to end of row. From now on continue to follow chart to end and fasten off thread.

EDGING—Working from right side, make a loop on hook and beginning in 3rd space before a corner space on long side of piece, work 3 s c in each of the 3 spaces to corner space, † 9 s c in corner space, * 3 s c in each of the next 6 spaces, 4 s c in next space; repeat from * 3 times, 3 s c in each of the next 7 spaces to corner, 9 s c in corner space, * 3 s c in each of the next 6 spaces, 2 s c in next space; repeat from last * 7 times, 3 s c in each of the next 3 spaces to corner, then repeat from † along remaining 2 sides of piece, end with last decrease on long side of piece, join with a slip st in first st of round. **2nd round:** ch 1, 1 s c in next st, * ch 1, skip 1 st, 1 s c in next st; repeat from * 5 times, ch 1, 1 more s c in same st (corner), ch 1, skip 1 st, 1 s c in next st. **1st row of corner scallop:** ch 2, turn, 1 d c in corner space, ch 2 and a 2nd d c in same space, ch 2, a 3rd d c in same space, ch 2, skip 1 space on edge, 1 s c in next space. † **2nd row:** turn, work 1 s c in first space, * ch 4, slip st in 4th st from hook (picot), 1 s c in same space, 1 s c in top of next d c, 1 s c in next space; repeat from * twice, ch 4, picot, 1 s c in same space, skip 1 st on edge, 1 s c in next st, ch 1, skip 1 st on edge, 1 s c in next st. **3rd row:** ch 5, turn, work 1 d c in center s c between the first 2 picots, ch 5, 1 d c in center s c between next 2 picots, ch 5, 1 d c in center s c between next 2 picots, ch 5, skip next space on edge, 1 s c in next space. **4th row:** turn, work 4 s c in first space, ch 4, picot, 4 more s c in same space, * 1 s c in top of next d c, work a group

(continued on next page)

Charts for "Rose Filet" Luncheon Set

PLACE MAT

SCARF

(continued)

of 4 s c, ch 4, picot, 4 more s c,—all in next space; repeat from * twice, skip 1 st on edge, work 1 s c in next st, ch 1, skip next st on edge, 1 s c in next st. **5th row:** ch 9, turn, work 1 d c in center s c between the first 2 picots of row below, ch 9 and 1 d c in center s c between the next 2 picots, ch 9 and 1 d c in center s c between the next 2 picots, ch 9, skip 1 space on edge, work 1 s c in next space. **6th row:** turn, work 4 s c in first space, * ch 4, picot, 4 s c in same space, ch 4, picot, 4 more s c in same space, ch 4, picot, 4 s c in next space; repeat from * twice, ch 4, picot, 4 s c in same space, ch 4, picot, 4 more s c in same space, skip 1 st on edge, work 1 s c in next st. This completes a corner scallop, * ch 1, skip 1 st on edge, work 1 s c in next st; repeat from * 9 times. **1st row of next scallop:** ch 2, turn, skip 1 space, work 1 d c in next space, ch 2, 1 d c in same space, ch 2, 1 more d c in same space, ch 2, skip next space, 1 s c in next space; repeat from † to next corner, work a corner scallop same as first corner, then continue around working all corners alike, end with ch 1, join with a slip st in first s c of round and fasten off thread. Tack the 2 end picots of scallops together as shown in illustration. This completes one place mat, make 3 more of these mats.

SCARF—Following the directions for place mat, follow the chart for scarf to end.

EDGING—Working from right side and beginning in 3rd space before corner space on long side of scarf, work 3 s c in each of the 3 spaces to corner, † 9 s c in corner space, * 3 s c in each of the next 6 spaces, 4 s c in next space; repeat from * 3 times, 3 s c in each of the remaining 7 spaces to corner, 9 s c in corner space, * 3 s c in each of the next 14 spaces, 4 s c in next space; repeat from last * 6 times, 3 s c in each of the remaining 8 spaces to next corner; then repeat from † to end of round, thus working along other 2 sides of scarf in same way and join as before. From now on follow the directions for edging of place mat, beginning with the 2nd round to end. Darn in all ends neatly.

Double Feature

MATERIALS:

J. & P. COATS KNIT-CRO-SHEEN, 4 balls of White or Ecru are sufficient for 2 Place Mats, each about 12½ x 16½ inches, and a runner, about 12½ x 24 inches.

Steel Crochet Hook No. 6 or 7.

PLACE MAT . . . Ch 139 to measure 15 inches. **1st row:** Sc in 14th ch from hook, sc in next ch, * ch 6, skip 3 ch, tr in next 2 ch, ch 6, skip 3 ch, sc in next 2 ch. Repeat from * across, ending with ch 6, skip 3 ch, tr in last ch. Ch 1, turn. **2nd row:** Sc in tr, * ch 6, sc in next 2 sc, ch 6, sc in next 2 tr. Repeat from * across, ending with ch 6, skip 6 sts of turning chain, sc in next ch. Ch 18, turn. **3rd row:** * Skip next 2 sc, tr in next 2 sc, ch 14. Repeat from * across, ending with ch 14, skip next 2 sc, tr in last sc. Ch 1, turn. **4th row:** Sc in 1st tr, * ch 6, skip 6 sts of next ch-14, sc in next 2 ch, ch 6, sc in next 2 tr. Repeat from * across, ending with ch 6, skip 6 sts of turning chain, sc in next 2 ch, ch 6, skip 6 more sts of turning chain, sc in next ch. Ch 7, turn. **5th row:** Skip 1st sc, * ch 3, sc in next 2 sc, ch 3, tr in next 2 sc. Repeat from * across, ending with ch 3, tr in last sc. Ch 1, turn. **6th row:** Sc in tr, * ch 3, sc in next 2 sc, ch 3, sc in next 2 tr. Repeat from * across, ending with ch 3, skip 3 ch, sc in next ch. Ch 10, turn. **7th row:** * Sc in next 2 sc, ch 6, tr in next 2 sc, ch 6. Repeat from * across, ending with ch 6, tr in last sc. Ch 1, turn. Repeat 2nd to 7th rows incl 4 more times; then repeat 2nd to 5th rows incl once more.

Now work Border as follows: **1st rnd:** Ch 3, 4 dc in tr just made, * 3 dc in next sp, dc at ends of each of next 2 chains. Repeat from * across narrow edge of mat. Make 5 dc in corner, ** 3 dc in next sp, dc in same place as next 2 sc. Repeat from ** across wide edge of mat. Complete remaining edges to correspond. Join with sl st in 3rd st of starting chain. **2nd rnd:** Ch 3, dc in next dc, * 5 dc in next dc, dc in each dc across to center dc of next corner. Repeat from * around. Join. **3rd rnd:** Ch 4, tr in 3 dc, ** make 5 tr in corner dc, tr in next 4 dc, * ch 6, skip 3 dc, sc in next 2 dc, ch 6, skip 3 dc, tr in next 2 dc. Repeat from * across to 7 sts from corner dc, skip 3 dc, tr in next 4 dc. Repeat from ** around, joining last ch-6 with sl st in 4th st of starting chain. **4th rnd:** Ch 1, sc in same place as sl st, sc in next 5 tr, ** 3 sc in corner tr, sc in next 6 tr, * ch 6, sc in next 2 sc, ch 6, sc in next 2 tr. Repeat from * across to next corner, sc in next 6 tr. Repeat from ** around. Join. **5th rnd:** ** Sc in each sc to corner sc, in corner sc make sc, ch 5 and sc; sc in each sc to next chain, * sc in each ch, sc in 2 sc, sc in each ch, sc in next sc, ch 5, sc in next sc. Repeat from * across to next corner. Repeat from ** around. Break off.

RUNNER . . . Ch 89 to measure 10 inches. Work 1st to 7th rows incl same as Place Mat. Repeat 2nd to 7th rows incl 11 more times; then repeat 2nd to 5th rows incl once more. Work Border same as Border of Place Mat. Starch, pin out to measurement and press.

Double Feature

Fisherman's Lace

Fisherman's Lace

MATERIALS:

J. & P. COATS or CLARK'S O.N.T. BEST SIX CORD MERCERIZED CROCHET, *Size 30.*

SMALL BALL:

J. & P. COATS —5 balls of White or Ecru, or 6 balls of any color,

OR

CLARK'S O.N.T.—7 balls of White or Ecru, or 9 balls of any color.

BIG BALL:

J. & P. COATS —3 balls of White, Ecru or Cream.

Steel Crochet Hook No. 10 or 11.

3/4 yard of linen.

This material is sufficient to make 2 place mats each about 11 1/2 x 16 1/2 inches, a runner about 11 1/2 x 22 inches and 2 napkins about 11 inches square.

PLACE MAT—Lace . . . Make a chain 1 yard long (14 ch sts to 1 inch). **1st rnd:** In 6th ch from hook make tr, ch 1 and tr, (ch 1, skip next ch, tr in next ch) 38 times; ch 1, skip next ch, in next ch make (tr, ch 1) twice and tr; (ch 1, skip next ch, tr in next ch) 74 times; ch 1, skip next ch, in next ch make (tr, ch 1) twice and tr; (ch 1, skip next ch, tr in next ch) 38 times; ch 1, skip next ch, in next ch make (tr, ch 1) twice and tr; (ch 1, skip next ch, tr in next ch) 74 times; ch 1, join with sl st in 4th st of turning chain at beginning of rnd. Cut off remaining chain. **2nd rnd:** Ch 5, ** in corner tr make (tr, ch 1) twice and tr; * ch 1, tr in next tr. Repeat from * across to next corner tr, ch 1. Repeat from ** around. Join. **3rd to 7th rnds incl:** Ch 5, * make tr in next tr, ch 1. Repeat from * across to next corner tr; in corner tr make (tr, ch 1) twice and tr. Continue thus around. Join. **8th rnd:** Ch 7, skip next tr, tr in next tr, (ch 3, skip next tr, tr in next tr) twice; ch 3, in corner tr make (tr, ch 1) twice and tr; ch 3, tr in next tr, (ch 3, skip next tr, tr in next tr) 21 times; (ch 1, tr in next tr) 3 times; (ch 3, skip next tr, tr in next tr) 21 times; ch 3, in corner tr make (tr, ch 1) twice and tr; ch 3, tr in next tr, (ch 3, skip next tr, tr in next tr) 12 times; (ch 1, tr in next tr) 3 times; (ch 3, skip next tr, tr in next tr) 12 times; ch 3, in corner tr make (tr, ch 1) twice and tr; ch 3, tr in next tr, (ch 3, skip next tr, tr in next tr) 21 times; (ch 1, tr in next tr) 3 times; (ch 3, skip next tr, tr in next tr) 21 times; ch 3, in corner tr make (tr, ch 1) twice and tr; ch 3, tr in next tr, (ch 3, skip next tr, tr in next tr) 12 times; (ch 1, tr in next tr) 3 times; (ch 3, skip next tr, tr in next tr) 8 times. Ch 3 and join with sl st in 4th st of starting chain.

9th and 10th rnds: Ch 7 and work in pattern as established on 8th rnd, making ch-3 sps over ch-3 sps and ch-1 sps over ch-1 sps and turning corners as before. Join. **11th rnd:** Ch 7, (tr in next tr, tr in next 3 ch, tr in next tr, ch 3) twice; tr in next tr, tr in 3 ch, tr in next tr, ch 3, in corner tr make (tr, ch 1) twice and tr; ch 3, (tr in next tr, tr in 3 ch, tr in next tr, ch 3) 12 times; (tr in next tr, tr in next ch) 3 times; tr in next tr, (ch 3, tr in next tr, tr in 3 ch, tr in next tr) 12 times; ch 3, in corner tr make (tr, ch 1) twice and tr, ch 3, (tr in next tr, tr in 3 ch, tr in next tr, ch 3) 15 times; tr in next tr, tr in 3 ch, tr in next tr, ch 3, turn corner as before and complete remaining two sides to correspond. Join. **12th rnd:** Ch 1, sc in same place as sl st, (ch 5, sc in 5th ch from hook—p made—sc in 3 ch, sc in next tr, p, sc in 4 tr) 3 times; sc in 3 ch, (p, sc in tr, sc in ch-1) twice; p, sc in tr, * sc in 3 ch, sc in next tr, p, sc in next 4 tr, p. Repeat from * around, turning corner as before. Join and break off. Press lace through damp cloth. Cut a paper pattern of the center area. Cut linen slightly larger than pattern (allowing for a narrow hem). Hem edges; then sew lace to linen.

RUNNER—Lace . . . Make a chain 1 1/2 yards long (14 ch sts to 1 inch). **1st rnd:** In 6th ch from hook make tr, ch 1 and tr, (ch 1, skip next ch, tr in next ch) 38 times; ch 1, skip next ch, in next ch make (tr, ch 1) twice and tr; (ch 1, skip next ch, tr in next ch) 118 times; ch 1, skip next ch, in next ch make (tr, ch 1) twice and tr; (ch 1, skip next ch, tr in next ch) 38 times; ch 1, skip next ch, in next ch make (tr, ch 1) twice and tr; (ch 1, skip next ch, tr in next ch) 118 times; ch 1, join with sl st in 4th st of turning chain at beginning of rnd. Cut off remaining chain. **2nd to 7th rnds incl:** Work same as 2nd to 7th rnds of Place Mat. **8th rnd:** Ch 7, skip next tr, tr in next tr, (ch 3, skip next tr, tr in next tr) twice; ch 3, in corner tr make (tr, ch 1) twice and tr; ch 3, tr in next tr, (ch 3, skip next tr, tr in next tr) 12 times; (ch 1, tr in next tr) 3 times; (ch 3, skip next tr, tr in next tr) 12 times; ch 3, in corner tr make (tr, ch 1) twice and tr; ch 3, tr in next tr, (ch 3, skip next tr, tr in next tr) 32 times; (ch 1, tr in next tr) 3 times; (ch 3, skip next tr, tr in next tr) 32 times; ch 3, in corner tr make (tr, ch 1) twice and tr; ch 3, tr in next tr, (ch 3, skip next tr, tr in next tr) 12 times; (ch 1, tr in next tr) 3 times; (ch 3, skip next tr, tr in next tr) 12 times; ch 3, in corner tr make (tr, ch 1) twice and tr; ch 3, tr in next tr, (ch 3, skip next tr, tr in next tr) 32 times; (ch 1, tr in next tr) 3 times; (ch 3, skip next tr, tr in next tr) 28 times. Ch 3 and join with sl st in 4th st of starting chain.

9th and 10th rnds: Work same as 9th and 10th rnds of Place Mat. **11th rnd:** Ch 7, (tr in next tr, tr in next 3 ch, tr in next tr, ch 3) twice; tr in next tr, tr in 3 ch, tr in next tr, ch 3, in corner tr make (tr, ch 1) twice and tr; (ch 3, tr in next tr, tr in 3 ch, tr in next tr) 8 times; ch 5, skip next 2 tr, (tr in next tr, tr in 3 ch, tr in next tr, ch 3) 8 times; in corner tr make (tr, ch 1) twice and tr; (ch 3, tr in next tr, tr in 3 ch, tr in next tr) 18 times; ch 5, skip 2 tr, (tr in next tr, tr in 3 ch, tr in next tr, ch 3) 18 times; turn corner and complete remaining two sides to correspond. Join. **12th rnd:** Work same as 12th rnd of Place Mat. Sew linen in center same as Place Mat.

NAPKIN—Lace . . . Make a chain 10 inches long (14 ch sts to 1 inch). **1st row:** Tr in 11th ch from hook, (ch 3, skip 3 ch, tr in next ch) 12 times; ch 3, skip next ch, in next ch make (tr, ch 1) twice and tr; ch 3, skip next ch, tr in next ch, (ch 3, skip 3 ch, tr in next ch) 13 times. Cut off remaining chain. Ch 7, turn. **2nd row:** (Tr in next tr, tr in 3 ch, tr in next tr, ch 3) 7 times; in corner tr make (tr, ch 1) twice and tr; (ch 3, tr in next tr, tr in 3 ch, tr in next tr) 7 times; ch 3, skip 3 sts of turning chain, tr in next ch. Break off.

Cut linen 11 1/2 inches square. Cut out corner for lace. Roll entire edge and whip down. Sew lace to edge of cut-out corner. Attach crochet thread in top of last tr made, make a chain about 5 inches long. Attach another ball of thread in same tr, ch 1 and work sc in each st of chain just made. Whip the chain edge of this strip to edge of napkin. * Make 5 inches more of chain; work sc in each st of chain; then whip to edge of napkin. Repeat from * until other end of corner is reached. Break off the chain thread and continue with sc over lace edge as follows: * Ch 5, sc in 5th ch from hook (p made), sc in 3 ch, sc in tr, p, sc in 4 tr. Repeat from * to corner; sc in 3 ch, sc in tr, p, (sc in ch 1, sc in tr, p) twice; ** sc in 3 ch, sc in tr, p, sc in 4 tr, p. Repeat from ** across to end of lace. Break off.

LAUREL This beautiful luncheon set will be handed down as an heirloom.

MATERIALS: For best results use—

CLARK'S O.N.T. OR J. & P. COATS
BEST SIX CORD MERCERIZED CROCHET, Size 20:

SMALL BALL:

CLARK'S O.N.T.—*18 balls of White or Ecru.*

OR

J. & P. COATS—*13 balls of White or Ecru.*

BIG BALL:

CLARK'S O.N.T. OR J. & P. COATS—*8 balls of White or Ecru.*

MILWARD'S *steel crochet hook No. 9.*

The above materials are sufficient for a set consisting of a centerpiece about 18 inches in diameter; 6 place doilies about 12½ inches in diameter; 6 bread and butter plate doilies, about 8 inches in diameter; and 6 glass doilies, about 6 inches in diameter.

GLASS DOILY *(Make 6)*...Ch 12, join. **1st rnd:** Ch 6 (to count as tr and ch-2), * tr in ring, ch 2. Repeat from * 16 more times. Join with sl st to 4th ch of ch-6 first made. **2nd rnd:** S c in sp, * ch 3, s c in next sp. Repeat from * 16 more times, ch 1; d c in s c first made. **3rd rnd:** S c under d c, * ch 4, s c in next loop. Repeat from * around, ending with ch 2, d c in 1st s c. **4th rnd:** Same as 3rd rnd, but make ch-5 loops (instead of ch-4). **5th rnd:** Same as 4th rnd, but make ch-6 loops; end with ch 3, d c in s c. **6th rnd:** Same as 5th rnd, making ch-7 loops and ending with ch 3, tr in s c. **7th rnd:** Same as 6th rnd, making ch-8 loops and ending with ch 4, tr in s c. **8th rnd:** Same as 7th rnd, ending with ch 4, d tr in s c. **9th rnd:** Ch 5 (to count as d tr); 3 d tr at base of ch-5, holding back the last loop of each d tr on hook; thread over and draw through all loops on hook (a cluster), ch 1; 4 d tr in 4th ch of next ch-8 loop, holding back the last loop of each d tr on hook; thread over and complete a cluster as before, * ch 10, make another cluster in same ch as last cluster, ch 1, cluster in 4th ch of next loop. Repeat from * around, ending with cluster in same place as 1st cluster, ch 10, sl st in tip of 1st cluster. **10th rnd:** Sl st in next ch, s c in next ch; * (ch 5, skip 1 ch, s c in next ch) 3 times; ch 3, s c in 3rd ch of next loop. Repeat from * around. Join. **11th rnd:** Sl st in next 2 ch, s c in next ch; * (ch 7, s c in 3rd ch of next loop) twice, ch 5, skip ch-3, s c in 3rd ch of next loop. Repeat from * around. Join. **12th rnd:** Sl st in first 3 ch, s c in next ch, * ch 8, s c in 4th ch of next loop, ch 7, skip ch-5, s c in 4th ch of next loop. Repeat from * around. Join, fasten off.

BREAD AND BUTTER PLATE DOILY *(Make 6)*... Work 1st 8 rnds as for Glass Doily. **9th rnd:** Same as 9th rnd of Glass Doily, making ch-12 loops (instead of ch-10). **10th rnd:** S c between 2 clusters, * ch 13, skip loop, s c between next 2 clusters. Repeat from * around. Join with sl st. **11th rnd:** Sl st in next 6 ch, s c over ch-13 loop and in 7th ch of ch-12 loop of 9th rnd, * ch 15, s c in 7th ch of next ch-12 loop of 9th rnd, working over the ch-13 loop of 10th rnd. Repeat from * around, ending with ch 15, sl st in s c. **12th rnd:** Sl st in next 3 ch, s c in next ch; * (ch 5, skip 1 ch, s c in next ch) 4 times; ch 4, s c in 4th ch of next loop. Repeat from * around. Join with sl st. **13th rnd:** Sl st in 1st 2 ch, s c in next ch, * (ch 7, s c in 3rd ch of next loop) 3 times; ch 5, skip the ch-4, s c in 3rd ch of next loop. Repeat from * around, join. **14th rnd:** Sl st in 1st 3 ch, s c in next ch; * (ch 7, s c in 4th ch of next loop) twice; ch 7, skip the ch-5, s c in 4th ch of next loop. Repeat from * around. Join. **15th rnd:** Sl st in 1st 3 ch, s c in next ch, * ch 8, s c in 4th ch of next loop, ch 10, skip ch-7, s c in 4th ch of next loop. Repeat from * around. Join and fasten off.

PLACE DOILY *(Make 6)*... Work 1st 15 rnds as for Bread and Butter Plate Doily, but do not fasten off. **16th rnd:** Sl st in 1st 3 ch, s c in loop, * ch 9, s c in next loop. Repeat from * around, ending with ch 5, d tr in s c first made. **17th rnd:** Ch 5 (to count as d tr) and make a cluster at base of ch-5, * ch 1, cluster in 5th ch of next loop, ch 12, another cluster in same ch as last cluster. Repeat from * around, ending with ch 12, sl st in tip of 1st cluster. **18th to 23rd rnds incl:** Repeat 10th to 15th rnds incl. of Bread and Butter Plate Doily. Fasten off.

CENTERPIECE... Work 1st 23 rnds as for Place Doily, but do not fasten off. **24th, 25th and 26th rnds:** Repeat 16th, 17th and 18th rnds of Place Doily. **27th rnd:** Sl st in next 6 ch, s c over ch-13 loop and into 7th ch of ch-12 loop of 25th rnd; * ch 13, s c in 7th ch of next ch-12 loop of 25th rnd, working over the ch-13 loop of 26th rnd. Repeat from * around, ending with ch 13, sl st in s c. **28th rnd:** Sl st in next 2 ch, s c in next ch; * (ch 5, skip 1 ch, s c in next ch) 4 times; ch 2, s c in 3rd ch of next loop. Repeat from * around. Join with sl st. **29th rnd:** Sl st in 1st 2 ch, s c in next ch; * (ch 7, s c in 3rd ch of next loop) 3 times; ch 3, skip ch-2, s c in 3rd ch of next loop. Repeat from * around; join. **30th rnd:** Sl st in 1st 3 ch, s c in next ch; * (ch 7, s c in 4th ch of next loop) twice; ch 4, skip ch-3, s c in 4th ch of next loop. Repeat from * around; join. **31st rnd:** Sl st in 1st 3 ch, s c in next ch, * ch 8, s c in 4th ch of next loop, ch 5, skip ch-4, s c in 4th ch of next loop. Repeat from * around. Join and fasten off.

Aristocrat Luncheon Set

MATERIALS: *11 balls Cynthia Mercerized Crochet Cotton, size 20, White or Ecru.*

Milward's Crochet Hook No. 12.

Buy Sufficient Material at one time.

Set is composed of a center runner, 15½ x 27 inches, and 4 place mats, 12½ x 17 inches.

RUNNER

Ch 166 sts, turn. **1st row:** Work 1 D C in 7th ch from hook, * ch 2, skip 2 ch, 1 D C in next ch, repeat from * 52 times, ch 5, turn. **2nd row:** 1 D C in first D C, * ch 2, skip the ch 2 on previous row, 1 D C in next D C, repeat from * 51 times, ch 2, skip 2 ch, 1 D C in next ch, ch 5, turn. **3rd row:** 1 D C in first D C, ch 2, skip the ch 2 on previous row, * 1 D C in next D C, 2 D C in mesh, repeat from * 49 times, 1 D C in next D C, ch 2, skip 2 ch, 1 D C in next D C, ch 2, skip 2 ch, 1 D C in next ch, ch 5, turn. **4th row:** 1 D C in first D C, ch 2, skip 2 ch, 1 D C in each of next 151 sts, ch 2, 1 D C in next D C, ch 2, 1 D C in 3rd ch of previous row, ch 5, turn. **5th-15th rows, inclusive:** same as 4th row. **16th row:** 1 D C in first D C, ch 2, skip 2 ch, 1 D C in each of next 34 sts, * ch 2, skip 2 sts, 1 D C in next D C, repeat from * 27 times, 1 D C in each of next 33 sts, ch 2, skip 2 ch, 1 D C in next D C, ch 2, skip 2 ch, 1 D C in next ch, ch 5, turn. **17th-21st rows, inclusive:** same as 16th row. **22nd row:** 1 D C in first D C, ch 2, skip 2 ch, 1 D C in each of next 34 sts, * ch 2, skip 2 ch, 1 D C in next D C, repeat from * 5 times, ** 2 D C in mesh, 1 D C in next D C, repeat from ** 15 times. *** ch 2, skip 2 ch, 1 D C in next D C, repeat from *** 5 times, 1 D C in each of next 33 sts, ch 2, skip 2 ch, 1 D C in next D C, ch 2, skip 2 ch, 1 D C in next ch, ch 5, turn. **23rd-95th rows, inclusive:** same as 22nd row. **96th-101st rows, inclusive:** same as 16th-21st rows. **102nd-114th rows, inclusive:** same as 3rd-15th rows. **115th-116th rows:** same as 1st and 2nd rows, but ch 4 only at end of 116th row, turn, 1 S C in 1st mesh, * ch 4, 1 S C in next mesh, repeat from * throughout entire piece working ch 4, 1 S C twice in corner meshes instead of once.

EDGING: Ch 15, turn.

1st row: 1 TR in 11th ch from hook, ch 3, skip 3 ch, 1 TR in next ch, ch 8, turn. **2nd row:** 1 TR in 1st TR, ch 8, skip 3 ch, 1 S C in next ch. **3rd row:** Work 9 S C in each mesh. Join round with slip st. **4th row:** * Ch 7, skip 4 S C, 1 S C in next S C, ch 7, skip 3 S C, 1 S C in next S C. Repeat from * 3 times. Join round with slip st. **5th row:** * Work 6 S C in next loop, ch 3, 6 S C in same loop, repeat from * 5 times. Work 6 S C in next loop, ch 1, slip st in 4-ch loop around edge of large piece, ch 1, 6 S C in same loop, 6 S C in next loop, ch 1, skip 2 loops on large piece, slip st in next loop, ch 1, 6 S C in same loop, join round with slip st.

When working other motifs, attach same next to each other on runner, skipping two 4-ch loops and join the small motifs to each other by joining the two corresponding loops of each in same manner; at corners join only 1 loop instead of two.

PLACE MAT

Ch 124 sts, turn. **1st row:** Work 1 D C in 7th ch from hook, * ch 2, skip 2 ch, 1 D C in next ch, repeat from * 38 times, ch 5, turn. **2nd row:** 1 D C in first D C,* ch 2, skip the ch 2 on previous row, 1 D C in next D C. Repeat from * 37 times, ch 2, skip 2 ch, 1 D C in next ch, ch 5, turn. **3rd row:** 1 D C in first D C, ch 2, skip the ch 2 on previous row, * 1 D C in next D C, 2 D C in mesh, repeat from * 35 times, 1 D C in next D C, ch 2, skip 2 ch, 1 D C in next D C, ch 2, skip 2 ch, 1 D C in next ch, ch 5, turn. **4th row:** 1 D C in first D C, ch 2, skip 2 ch, 1 D C in each of next 109 sts, ch 2, skip 2 ch, 1 D C in next D C, ch 2, skip 2 ch, 1 D C in next ch, ch 5, turn. **5th-12th rows, inclusive:** same as 4th row. **13th row:** 1 D C in next D C, ch 2, skip 2 ch, 1 D C in each of next 25 sts, * ch 2, skip 2 sts, 1 D C in next st, repeat from * 19 times, 1 D C in each of next 24 sts, ch 2, skip 2 ch, 1 D C in next D C, ch 2, skip 2 ch, 1 D C in next ch, ch 5, turn. **14th-16th rows, inclusive:** same as 13th row. **17th row:** 1 D C in next D C, ch 2, skip 2 ch, 1 D C in each of next 25 sts, * ch 2, skip 2 ch, 1 D C in next D C, repeat from * 3 times, ** 2 D C in mesh, 1 D C in next D C, repeat from ** 11 times. *** ch 2, skip 2 ch, 1 D C in next D C, repeat from *** 3 times, 1 D C in each of next 24 sts, ch 2, skip 2 ch, 1 D C in next D C, ch 2, skip 2 ch, 1 D C in next ch, ch 5, turn. **18th-58th rows, inclusive:** same as 17th row. **59th-74th rows, inclusive:** same as 16th to 1st rows reversed, then ch 4, 1 S C in 1st mesh, * ch 4, 1 S C in next mesh, repeat from * throughout entire piece, working ch 4, 1 S C twice in corner meshes instead of once.
Work edging same as for runner.

Swirl Luncheon Set

MATERIALS: *7 balls Cynthia Mercerized Crochet Cotton, White or Ecru, size 10.*

Boye Steel Crochet Hook No. 6.

Buy Sufficient Thread at one time.

Set is composed of four 11½-inch plate mats, four 6-inch butter plate mats, four 5½-inch tumbler mats and a 14-inch center mat.

PLATE MAT

Ch 5, join to form a ring. **1st round:** * ch 6, 1 S C in ring, repeat from * 4 times, join round with slip st. **2nd round:** * ch 6, skip 3 chs of ch-6 loop, 1 S C in each of last 3 chs, repeat from * 4 times. **3rd round:** Ch 6, * skip 3 chs, 1 S C in each of 3 chs, 1 S C in each of 2 S C, ch 6, (skipping last S C), repeat from * 4 times. Repeat 3rd round, always working 3 S C in last 3 chs of ch-6 loop, 1 S C in each S C, always skipping the last S C until there are 25 S C in each of the 5 groups. **Next round:** * ch 5, 1 S C in 3rd ch of ch-6 loop,

(continued on page 40)

Empress Luncheon Set

MATERIALS: *9 balls Cynthia Mercerized Crochet Cotton, size 20, White or Ecru.*

Boye Steel Crochet Hook No. 8.

Buy Sufficient Thread at one time.

Set consists of 4 place mats about 12 x 17 inches and a runner about 13¼ x 27 inches.

PLACE MAT

Ch 113 sts, turn. 1st row: 3 TR in 5th ch from hook, * skip 4 chs, 4 TR in the next ch, ch 5, skip

(continued on page 40)

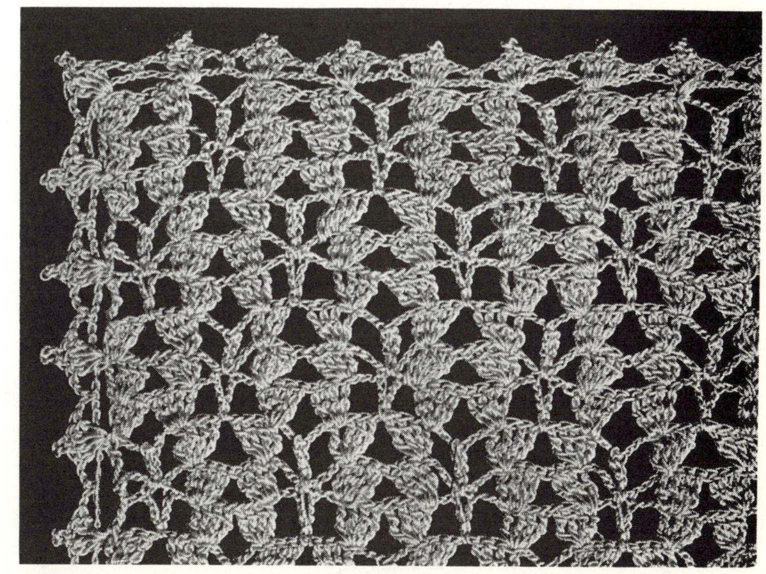

Swirl Luncheon Set

(continued from page 38)

ch 5, skip 1 S C, 1 S C in each of the next 23 S C, skip the last S C, repeat from * 5 times.
Repeat previous round with 1 less S C each side of group each round and 1 more loop between each 2 S C groups until there are 3 S C and 12 loops in each section. **Next round:** After the S C in the last loop of section, * ch 3, 1 D C in 2nd S C of S C group, ch 3, 1 S C in next loop, 1 ch-5 loop in each of the next 11 loops, repeat from * around. **Next round:** * 1 D C in ch-3 loop, ch 5, 1 D C in next ch-3 loop, ch-5 loop in each of the next 11 loops, ch 5, repeat from * around. **Next 2 rounds:** Ch-5 loop in each ch-5 loop. **Next 3 rounds:** Ch-6 loop in each ch-5 loop. **Next 3 rounds:** Ch-7 loop in each ch-6 loop. **Final round:** same as previous round. Join with slip st and fasten off.

BUTTER PLATE MAT

Work the same as plate mat until there are 13 S C in each group, then decrease until there are 3 S C and 6 loops in each section.
Next round: After the S C in the last loop, * ch 3, 1 D C in 2nd S C of S C group, ch 3, 1 S C in next loop, 1 loop in each of the next 5 loops, repeat from * around. **Next round:** * 1 D C in ch-3 loop, ch 5, 1 D C in next ch-3 loop, ch-5 loop in each of the next 5 loops, ch 5, repeat from * around. **Next 2 rounds:** Ch-5 loop in each ch-5 loop. **Next 2 rounds:** Ch-6 loop in each ch-5 loop. **Final round:** ch-6 loop in each ch-6 loop, join and fasten off.

TUMBLER MAT

Work the same as butter plate mat until there are 11 S C and 5 loops in each section, then work remainder of mat in same manner as before, until mat measures 5½ inches. Join and fasten off.

CENTER MAT

Work the same as plate mat, working 5 more rounds of ch-7 loops or until mat measures 14 inches. Join and fasten off.

Empress Luncheon Set

(continued from page 39)

3 chs, 1 S C in the next ch, ch 5, skip 3 ch, 4 TR in the next ch, repeat from * 7 times, skip 3 chs, 4 TR in the last ch, ch 3, turn. **2nd row:** 3 TR in 1st TR, * 4 TR in the 8th TR, ch 3, 1 S C in the 3rd ch of ch-5, 1 S C in 3rd ch of the next ch-5, ch 3, 4 TR in the 1st TR of the next group of TR, repeat from * 7 times, 4 TR in last TR, ch 3, turn. **3rd row:** 3 TR in the 1st TR, * 4 TR in the 8th TR, ch 5, 1 S C between the 1st and 2nd S C on 2nd row, ch 3, join with slip st in 3rd ch of ch-5 just made, ch 3, 4 TR in the 1st TR of next group, repeat from * 7 times, 4 TR in the last TR, ch 8, turn. **4th row:** * 1 S C between the 1st and 2nd groups of TR, ch 5, 4 TR in last TR of 2nd group, 4 TR in 1st TR of next group, ch 5, repeat from * 7 times, 1 TR in the last TR, ch 5, turn. **5th row:** 1 S C in 3rd ch of first ch-5, 1 S C in 3rd ch of next ch-5, ch 3, * 4 TR in the 1st TR, 4 TR in the last TR of next group, ch 3, 1 S C in 3rd ch of next ch-5, 1 S C in 3rd ch of next ch-5, ch 3, repeat from * 7 times, 1 TR in 3rd ch of ch 8, ch 8, turn. **6th row:** 1 S C between the 1st and 2nd S C, ch 3, join with slip st in 3rd ch of ch 8, ch 3, * 4 TR in first TR of first group, 4 TR in last TR of next group, ch 5, 1 S C between next 2 S C, ch 3, join with slip st in 3rd ch of ch-5, ch 3, repeat from * 7 times, 1 TR in 3rd ch of ch-5 of last row.
Repeat rows 1–6 ten times (approximately 16½ inches), fasten off.

EDGING — **1st row:** Attach thread and * work 1 S C in first TR on corner, ch 7, 1 S C in 8th TR, repeat from * around mat. **2nd row:** 2 D C in S C on corner, ch 4, join with slip st in top of last D C just made (picot), 2 more D C in same space as first 2 D C, ch 2, 1 S C in 4th ch of first ch-7, ch 2, * 2 D C in S C of 1st row, ch 4, join with slip st in top of last D C just made, 2 D C in same space as first 2 D C, ch 2, 1 S C in 4th ch of next ch-7, ch 2, repeat from * around entire mat, join in top of 1st D C. Fasten off.

CENTER RUNNER

Ch 126 sts and work same as place mat, repeating pattern 17 times.

Southern Beau

Place Mats measure 12½ x 17 inches
Runner measures 12½ x 27 inches

DIRECTIONS ON PAGE 42

Southern Beau

ILLUSTRATED ON PAGE 41

MATERIALS:

J. & P. COATS KNIT-CRO-SHEEN, 3 balls of White or Ecru and 2 balls of any color are sufficient for 2 place mats, each about 12½ x 17 inches, and a runner about 12½ x 27 inches.

Steel Crochet Hook No. 6 or 7.

PLACE MAT . . . With White, ch 144 to measure 16¼ inches. **1st row:** Sc in 12th ch from hook, * ch 7, skip 3 ch, sc in next ch. Repeat from * across. Ch 10, turn. **2nd row:** * Sc in center st of next ch-7 loop, ch 7. Repeat from * across, ending with ch 7, skip 3 sts of turning chain, sc in next ch. Ch 10, turn. Repeat 2nd row until 30 rows in all are made. Ch 7, turn. **Next row:** * Sc in center st of next ch-7 loop, ch 3. Repeat from * across, ending with ch 3, skip 3 sts of turning chain, sc in next ch. Break off.

BORDER . . . 1st rnd: Attach color in center ch st of any corner, ch 1, work 3 sc in same place where thread was attached, sc in each ch and in each sc around, making 3 sc in each corner. Join with sl st in 1st sc made. **2nd rnd:** Sc in each sc around, making 3 sc in center sc of each corner. Join and break off. **3rd rnd:** Attach White in any corner sc, ch 1, in same place where thread was attached make sc, ch 7 and sc; * ch 7, skip 3 sc, sc in next sc. Repeat from * to next corner, in corner sc make sc, ch 7 and sc. Continue thus around. Join. **4th rnd:** Sl st in 3 ch of corner loop, ** in corner loop make sc, ch 7 and sc; * ch 7, sc in center st of next ch-7 loop. Repeat from * to next corner loop. Repeat from ** around. Join and break off. **5th rnd:** Attach color and work sl st in each ch st and in each sc of 4th rnd. Break off.

BOW . . . With color make a chain 40 inches long. **1st row:** Sc in 2nd ch from hook, sc in each ch across. Ch 1, turn. **2nd row:** Sc in each sc across. Break off. Make a bow of this piece. Pin mat out to measurements. Sew bow in place as illustrated.

RUNNER . . . With White, ch 100 to measure 11½ inches. Work same as Place Mat until 68 rows are completed. Ch 7, turn and work last row of Place Mat. Now work Border same as Border of Place Mat.

Make 2 Bows (make chains 30 inches long) and sew at each end of Runner.

Starch, pin out to measurements and press.

Spider Web

MATERIALS:

J. & P. COATS or CLARK'S O.N.T. BEST SIX CORD MERCERIZED CROCHET, *Size 30.*

SMALL BALL:

J. & P. COATS —7 balls of White or Ecru, or 9 balls of any color,

OR

CLARK'S O.N.T.—11 balls of White or Ecru, or 13 balls of any color.

BIG BALL:

J. & P. COATS —4 balls of White, Ecru or Cream.

Steel Crochet Hook No. 10.

Centerpiece measures about 17 inches in diameter and each place mat about 13 inches in diameter.

CENTERPIECE . . . Starting at center, ch 8. Join with sl st to form ring. **1st rnd:** Ch 5, * dc in ring, ch 2. Repeat from * 8 more times. Join last ch-2 with sl st to 3rd st of ch-5 first made (10 sps). **2nd rnd:** Ch 17, sl st in 8th ch from hook, make 4 sc in ring just made, * ch 4, 4 sc in ring. Repeat from * 2 more times. Join with sl st to 1st sc made, ch 9, sc in next dc, ** ch 17, sl st in 8th ch from hook, make 4 sc in ring, ch 2, sl st in adjacent ch-4 loop of previous ring, ch 2, 4 sc in 2nd ring (thus joining second ring to first), complete this ring as before, ch 9, sc in next dc. Repeat from ** around. Join last sc ring to previous ring and to first ring made. Join last ch-9 with sl st to base of starting chain (10 sc rings). Break off. **3rd rnd:** Attach thread to center of ch-4 loop, sc in same loop, ** ch 14, sl st in 8th ch from hook, 4 sc in ring just made, * ch 4, 4 sc in ring. Repeat from * 2 more times, join with sl st to 1st sc made, ch 6, dc in joining (between rings), ch 14, sl st in 8th ch from hook and complete another ring as before, joining to previous ring; ch 6, sc in next ch-4 loop. Repeat from ** around, joining last ring at both sides, and joining last ch-6 with sl st in 1st sc made. Break off. **4th rnd:** Attach thread to ch-4 loop, ch 14 (to count as dc and ch-11), * dc in next ch-4 loop, ch 11. Repeat from * around, joining last ch-11 with sl st to 3rd st of ch-14 first made.

5th rnd: Ch 4, * skip 1 ch, dc in next ch, ch 1. Repeat from * 4 more times, ch 1, skip 1 ch, dc in next dc and continue thus around, joining last ch-1 with sl st to 3rd st of ch-4 first made (120 sps). **6th rnd:** Sc in same place as sl st, ch 6 (to count as tr tr), in sc make 3 tr tr, always holding back the last loop of each tr tr; then thread over hook and draw through all loops on hook, ch 1 (thus making a 4-tr tr cluster). Make another 4-tr tr cluster, * skip 6 sps, sc in next dc, make 2 clusters. Repeat from * around, joining last cluster with sl st to 1st sc made. **7th rnd:** Ch 12 (to count as tr tr and ch-6), cluster in 6th ch from hook, * d tr between 2 clusters of previous rnd, cluster, tr tr in next sc, cluster. Repeat from * around. Join with sl st. **8th rnd:** Ch 12, cluster in 6th ch from hook, * d tr between 2 clusters of previous rnd, cluster, tr tr in next tr tr, cluster. Repeat from * around. Join with sl st. Break off.

Small Motif . . . 1st rnd: Ch 6, dc in 6th ch from hook, * ch 3, dc in same ch. Repeat from * 2 more times. Ch 3, join with sl st to 3rd st of ch-6 first made. **2nd rnd:** * 6 sc in sp, sc in dc. Repeat from * around. Join with sl st. **3rd rnd:** * Ch 5, skip 1 sc, sc in front loop of next sc. Repeat from * around. Join with sl st. **4th rnd:** Ch 5, sc in back loop of next sc, tr tr in tr tr of 8th rnd of Centerpiece, then make 2 more ch-5 loops as before, d tr in d tr (between clusters), 2 ch-5 loops, tr tr in next tr tr, and complete rnd (thus joining Small Motif to 8th rnd of Centerpiece). Break off. Make another Small Motif, joining to 8th rnd of Centerpiece as before and also joining to previous Small Motif at one side, having 2 ch-5 loops between joinings and making a tr tr to join. Continue in this manner around, joining last motif at both sides, thus completing the **9th rnd** of Centerpiece. **10th rnd:** Attach thread to 5th loop on Small Motif (counting from joining), sc in same loop, sc in next loop, * ch 18, skip 1 loop of same motif, d tr in next loop, ch 14, sl st in 14th ch from hook, d tr in 3rd loop of next motif, ch 18, skip 1 loop, sc in each of next 2 loops. Repeat from * around, ch 18, join with sl st to 1st sc made. Break off. **11th rnd:** Attach thread to ch-14 loop, sc in same loop, * ch 16, sc in next loop, ch 16, sc in next loop, ch 16, sc in next ch-14 loop. Repeat from * around. Join. **12th to 15th rnds incl:** Sl st to center of 1st loop, * ch 16, sc in next loop. Repeat from * around. Join. Break off.

PLACE DOILY (Make 4) . . . Starting at center, ch 8. Join with sl st to form ring. **1st and 2nd rnds:** Same as 1st and 2nd rnds of Centerpiece. **3rd rnd:** Attach thread to ch-4 loop, sc in same loop, * ch 14, sc in next ch-4 loop. Repeat from * around. Ch 14, join with sl st to sc first made. **4th rnd:** Ch 4, * skip 1 st, dc in next st, ch 1. Repeat from * around. Join (75 sps). **5th rnd:** Same as 6th rnd of Centerpiece, but skipping only 5 sps (instead of 6 sps). **6th to 13th rnds incl:** Same as 7th to 14th rnds incl of Centerpiece. Break off. Starch lightly and press.

Spider Web

Sun Porch

MATERIALS REQUIRED

American Thread Company "De Luxe" Mercerized Crochet and Knitting Cotton, 250 yard Balls.

No. 4 Beige, 6 Balls. No. 10 Lt. Green, 1 Ball.
No. 8 Maize, 1 Ball. No. 26-A Rust, 1 Ball.
Steel Crochet Hook #7.
Place Mats Measure, 10¼" x 14".
Center Scarf Measures, 11¼" x 26¼".

PLACE MATS. With Beige ch 105 and work 104 s c on ch.

2nd Row. Ch 1, turn, 1 s c in last s c of previous row, ch 2, skip 1 s c, s c in next s c, repeat from * across row ending with 2 s c. (Begin each row with ch 1 and 1 s c and end each row with 2 s c.) Repeat 2nd row until there are 100 rows.

101st Row. Ch 1, turn, 1 s c in last s c of previous row, 1 s c in next s c, * 1 s c in 2 ch loop, 1 s c in next s c, repeat from * across row and break thread.

Next row begins the stripe. Attach Henna, 1 s c in each s c, ch 2, turn.

2nd Row. 2 d c in first s c, skip 3 s c, s c in next s c, * ch 2, 2 d c in same space, skip 3 s c, s c in next s c repeat from * across row, ch 2, turn.

3rd Row. 2 d c in 1st s c, s c in ch of shell in previous row, * ch 2, 2 d c in same space, s c in ch of next shell, repeat from * across row and break thread. Work 1 row of shells in Beige, 2 rows in Lt. Green, 1 row in Beige, 2 rows in Maize, break thread and repeat stripe on other end of place mat. With Beige work a row of shells all around mat and work 1 row of shells in Henna across both ends. Work 3 more place mats to correspond.

CENTER SCARF. With Beige ch 113, work 112 s c on ch and work same as place mats for 43 rows, work 1 row of s c, break thread.

45th Row. Attach Henna, work 1 row of s c and 2 rows of shells. Work 1 row of shells in Beige, 2 rows Lt. Green, 1 row Beige, 2 rows Maize, 1 row Beige, 1 row Henna, ch 3, turn, * 1 s c in each d c of shell, 1 s c in ch of shell, ch 1, repeat from * across row, break thread. Attach Beige and work a row of s c (112 s c) ch 1, turn and repeat ch and s c pattern for 100

(continued on page 47)

Sun Ray

MATERIALS REQUIRED

American Thread Company "Star" Crochet Cotton Small Ball, Size 10

12 Balls Shade No. 111 Linen.
4 Balls Shade No. 127.5 Hunter Green.
4 Balls Shade No. 128.5 Henna.
Steel Crochet Hook #8.
Dimensions: Center Doily—14 inches, Plate Doily—11 inches, Small Doily—7½ inches.

CENTER DOILY—With Green, ch 8, join to form a ring, ch 1 and work 11 s c into ring, join each row.

2nd Row. Ch 8, 1 tr c in next st, * ch 3, 1 tr c in next st, repeat from * all around, ch 3 and join in 5th st of ch.

3rd Row. 4 s c over ch 3 and 1 s c in each tr c, break thread.

4th Row. Join Henna and work 1 s c in each s c, break thread.

5th Row. Join Green and repeat 4th row, break thread.

6th Row. Join Henna, ch 8, skip 1 s c, 1 tr c in next s c, * ch 3, skip 1 s c, 1 tr c in next s c, repeat from * all around, ch 3 join in 5th st of ch.

7th Row. 4 s c in each loop, break thread.

8th Row. Join Linen and work 1 s c in each s c then with Henna work 1 s c in each s c, break thread.

10th Row. Join Linen, ch 4, skip 1 st, d c in next st, ch 1, skip 1 st, d c in next st, * ch 3, skip 1 st, d c in next st, ch 1, skip 1 st, d c in next st, ch 1, skip 1 st, d c in next st, repeat from * all around, ch 3 and join.

11th Row. Same as 10th row.

12th Row. Sl st to ch between d c, d c in next mesh, ch 1, d c in 1st st of 3 ch loop, ch 3, d c in 3rd st of loop, ch 1, d c in next mesh and continue all around.

13th Row. Ch 4, d c in next d c, ch 1, d c in next d c, ch 1, d c in next d c, ch 3, d c in next d c and continue all around.

14th Row. Sl st to ch between d c and work same as 12th row, having 1 more mesh in each section.

15th Row. Same as 13th row. Continue work, hav-

(continued on page 47)

Wild Rose Luncheon Set

This mat may be made with any of the American Thread Company products listed below:

Material	Quantity	Size of Needle	Approx. Size of Mat
"STAR" Crochet Cotton Article 20, Size 30	8 Balls White 2 Balls each Green, Pink & Rose Pink 1 Ball Yellow	11 or 12	10½x16 inches
or			
"STAR" Crochet Cotton Article 30, Size 30	28 Balls White 4 Balls each Green, Pink & Rose Pink 1 Ball Yellow	11 or 12	10½x16½ inches
or			
"GEM" Crochet Cotton Article 35, Size 30	8 Balls White 2 Balls each Green, Pink & Rose Pink 1 Ball Yellow	11 or 12	10½x16½ inches
or			
"SILLATEEN SANSIL" Article 102	28 Balls White 4 Balls each Green, Pink & Rose Pink 1 Ball Yellow	10	12½x18½ inches

Will make 4 mats. Shaded Color may be used if desired.

With White ch 217, tr c in 12th st from hook, 1 tr c in next st of ch, * ch 3, skip 3 sts of ch, 1 tr c in each of the next 2 sts of ch, repeat from * 39 times, ch 3, skip 3 sts of ch, tr c in next st of ch, ch 1, turn.

2nd Row—S c in same space, * ch 3, 1 s c in each of the next 2 tr c, repeat from * across row ending row with ch 3, s c in 4th st of ch, ch 7, turn.

3rd Row—* 1 tr c in each of the next 2 s c, ch 3, repeat from * across row ending row with tr c in s c, ch 1, turn. Repeat the last 2 rows 22 times (piece should measure about 7¾ inches). Do not ch 1 to turn last row.

Next Row—Start border; working along side of work, ch 4, 3 tr c over side of tr c just made, * 1 tr c in side of each of the next 2 previous rows, 3 tr c in next mesh, repeat from * to corner mesh, work 7 more tr c in same mesh, 1 tr c in base of each of the next 2 tr c, continue working around remaining 3 sides in same manner ending row with 6 tr c in 1st mesh, join.

Next Row—Ch 7, skip 3 tr c, ** 1 tr c in each of the next 2 tr c, * ch 3, skip 3 tr c, 1 tr c in each of the next 2 tr c, repeat from * to next corner tr c group, ch 3, skip 3 tr c, 1 tr c in each of the next 2 tr c, ch 10, 1 tr c in each of the next 2 tr c, ch 3, skip 3 tr c, 1 tr c in each of the next 2 tr c, ch 3, repeat from ** all around in same manner ending row with ch 10, tr c in next st, join in 4th st of ch.

Next Row—Ch 1, s c in same space, * ch 3, 1 s c in each of the next 2 tr c, repeat from * to next corner loop, ch 3, skip 3 sts of ch, 1 s c in each of the next 4 sts of ch, repeat from 1st * all around in same manner, join in 1st s c.

Next Row—Ch 7, 1 tr c in each of the next 2 s c, * ch 3, 1 tr c in each of the next 2 s c, repeat from * to corner mesh, ch 3, 1 tr c in each of the next 2 s c, ch 10, 1 tr c in each of the next 2 s c, repeat from 1st * all around in same manner, join in 4th st of ch.

Repeat the last 2 rows 3 times.

(continued on page 47)

SUN PORCH

(continued from page 44)

rows, and work 1 row of s c. Attach Henna, work 1 row of s c and 1 row of shells, break thread. Work 1 row of shells in Beige, 2 rows Maize, 1 row Beige, 2 rows Lt. Green, 1 row Beige, 2 rows Henna, work 1 row of s c and break thread. Attach Beige and work 43 rows of ch and s c pattern, 1 row of s c, work a stripe at both ends same as place mats, work a row of shells all around in Beige and 1 row of shells in Henna across ends.

SUN RAY

(continued from page 45)

ing 1 more mesh in each section every other row until there are 20 rows of open meshes.

BORDER. With Henna, join thread in 3 ch loop and work 3 s c over ch, 1 s c in d c, 1 s c in next mesh and d c, skip next mesh, 1 s c in next d c, continue all around, skipping every other mesh.

2nd Row. With Green work 1 s c in each s c.

3rd Row. With Henna, work 1 s c in each s c, increasing 1 st in center s c over point.

4th Row. With Linen, ch 4, 2 d c in same st, ch 1, 3 d c in same st, * skip 2 s c, 1 s c in each of the next 17 s c, skip 2 sts, 3 d c, ch 1, 3 d c in next st, repeat from *.

5th Row. With Henna 1 s c in each st and 3 s c in each point.

6th Row. Attach Green in point, ch 4, sl st in first st for picot, 1 s c in each of the next 3 sts, picot, 1 s c in each s c to within 3 sts of point, picot, 1 s c in each of the next 3 sts, repeat all around.

PLATE DOILY. Work center and 14 rows of open meshes same as center doily and finish with border.

SMALL DOILY. Work center and 6 rows of open meshes and finish with border. If a larger center or daily is desired continue the rows of open meshes until size required. This set may also be made in any of the following threads—"Gem" Mercerized Crochet Cotton, "Star" Pearl Cotton size 5, "Star" Crochet Cord, "Gem" or "DeLuxe" Mercerized Crochet and Knitting Cotton.

WILD ROSE LUNCHEON SET

(continued from page 46)

Next Row—Ch 4, * 3 tr c in next mesh, 1 tr c in each of the next 2 tr c, repeat from * to next corner loop, 13 tr c in corner loop, repeat from 1st * all around in same manner, join in 4th st of ch.

Next Row—Ch 1, s c in same space, 1 s c in each of the next 9 tr c, ch 3, sl st in last s c for picot, * 1 s c in each of the next 10 tr c, ch 3, sl st in last s c for picot, repeat from * 12 times, * 1 s c in each of the next 5 tr c, ch 3 picot, repeat from * twice, * 1 tr c in each of the next 10 tr c, ch 3 picot, repeat from * 24 times, continue all around in same manner, join, break thread.

FLOWER—With Green ch 2 and work 10 s c in 2nd st from hook, join, break thread.

2nd Row—Attach Yellow, * ch 3, sl st in same space, ch 2, skip 1 s c, sl st in next s c, repeat from * 4 times, break thread.

Next Row—Petal; with wrong side of work toward you, attach Pink in any ch 2 loop and work 3 s c in loop, ch 1, turn.

Next 5 Rows—Working in s c, increase 1 s c at beginning and end of each row, ch 1 to turn each row. Work 1 row even, ch 3, turn.

Next Row—1 d c in same space, 1 d c in next s c, 1 s d c in next s c (s d c: thread over needle, insert in st, pull through, thread over and work off all loops at one time), 1 s c in each of the next 7 s c, 1 s d c in next s c, 1 d c in next s c, 2 d c in next s c, ch 3, turn.

Next Row—1 d c in each of the next 3 sts, 1 s d c in next st, 1 s c in each of the next 5 s c, 1 s d c in next st, 1 d c in each of the next 4 sts, ch 2, turn.

Next Row—1 d c in each of the next 4 sts, 1 s d c in next st, 1 s c in each of the next 3 sts, 1 s d c in next st, 1 d c in each of the next 4 sts, 1 s d c in next st, break thread. Work 4 more petals in same manner. Work 3 more flowers in same manner and 4 more flowers in Rose Pink.

LEAF—With Green ch 16, sl st in 2nd st from hook, 1 s c in each of the next 2 sts of ch, 1 s d c in each of the next 2 sts of ch, 1 d c in each of the next 5 sts of ch, 1 s d c in each of the next 2 sts of ch, 1 s c in each of the next 2 sts of ch, sl st in next st, working on opposite side of ch, 1 s c in each of the next 2 sts, 1 s d c in each of the next 2 sts, 1 d c in each of the next 5 sts, 1 s d c in each of the next 2 sts, 1 s c in each of the next 2 sts, sl st in next st, join in 1st sl st.

2nd Row—Sl st in each of the next 2 sts, 1 s c in each of the next 2 sts, 1 s d c in each of the next 5 sts, 1 s c in each of the next 2 sts, sl st in each of the next 5 sts, 1 s c in each of the next 2 sts, 1 s d c in each of the next 5 sts, 1 s c in each of the next 2 sts, sl st in remaining sts, join, ch 8, break thread leaving an end long enough for sewing. Work 7 more leaves in same manner. Work 18 more leaves in same manner omitting the ch 8 at end of each leaf.

FINISHING—Applique one Rose Pink flower in each corner. In two opposite corners applique one Pink flower on each side of Rose Pink flower as illustrated. Arrange and applique leaves as illustrated.

Simple Crochet Stitches

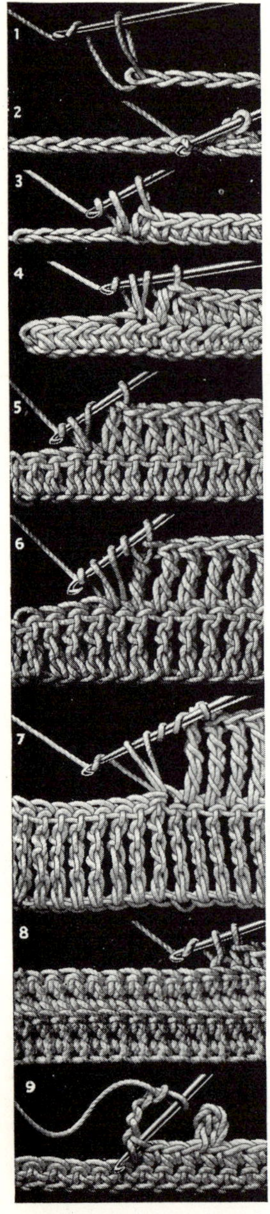

No. 1—Chain Stitch (CH) Form a loop on thread insert hook on loop and pull thread through tightening threads. Thread over hook and pull through last chain made. Continue chains for length desired.

No. 2—Slip Stitch (SL ST) Make a chain the desired length. Skip one chain, * insert hook in next chain, thread over hook and pull through stitch and loop on hook. Repeat from *. This stitch is used in joining and whenever an invisible stitch is required.

No. 3—Single Crochet (S C) Chain for desired length, skip 1 ch, * insert hook in next ch, thread over hook and pull through ch. There are now 2 loops on hook, thread over hook and pull through both loops, repeat from *. For succeeding rows of s c, ch 1, turn insert hook in top of next st taking up both threads and continue same as first row.

No. 4—Short Double Crochet (S D C) Ch for desired length thread over hook, insert hook in 3rd st from hook, draw thread through (3 loops on hook), thread over and draw through all three loops on hook. For succeeding rows, ch 2, turn.

No. 5—Double Crochet (D C) Ch for desired length, thread over hook, insert hook in 4th st from hook, draw thread through (3 loops on hook) thread over hook and pull through 2 loops thread over hook and pull through 2 loops. Succeeding rows, ch 3, turn and work next d c in 2nd d c of previous row. The ch 3 counts as 1 d c.

No. 6—Treble Crochet (TR C) Ch for desired length, thread over hook twice insert hook in 5th ch from hook draw thread through (4 loops on hook) thread over hook pull through 2 loops thread over, pull through 2 loops, thread over, pull through 2 loops. For succeeding rows ch 4, turn and work next tr c in 2nd tr c of previous row. The ch 4 counts as 1 tr c.

No. 7—Double Treble Crochet (D TR C) Ch for desired length thread over hook 3 times insert in 6th ch from hook (5 loops on hook) and work off 2 loops at a time same as tr c. For succeeding rows ch 5 turn and work next d tr c in 2nd d tr c of previous row. The ch 5 counts as 1 d tr c.

No. 8—Rib Stitch. Work this same as single crochet but insert hook in back loop of stitch only. This is sometimes called the slipper stitch.

No. 9—Picot (P) There are two methods of working the picot. (A) Work a single crochet in the foundation, ch 3 or 4 sts depending on the length of picot desired, sl st in top of s c made. (B) Work an s c, ch 3 or 4 for picot and s c in same space. Work as many single crochets between picots as desired.

No. 10—Open or Filet Mesh (O M.) When worked on a chain work the first d c in 8th ch from hook * ch 2, skip 2 sts, 1 d c in next st, repeat from *. Succeeding rows ch 5 to turn, d c in d c, ch 2, d c in next d c, repeat from *.

No. 11—Block or Solid Mesh (S M) Four double crochets form 1 solid mesh and 3 d c are required for each additional solid mesh. Open mesh and solid mesh are used in Filet Crochet.

No. 12—Slanting Shell St. Ch for desired length, work 2 d c in 4th st from hook, skip 3 sts, sl st in next st, * ch 3, 2 d c in same st with sl st, skip 3 sts, sl st in next st. Repeat from *. **2nd Row.** Ch 3, turn 2 d c in sl st, sl st in 3 ch loop of shell in previous row, * ch 3, 2 d c in same space, sl st in next shell, repeat from *.

No. 13—Bean or Pop Corn Stitch. Work 3 d c in same space, drop loop from hook insert hook in first d c made and draw loop through, ch 1 to tighten st.

No. 14—Cross Treble Crochet. Ch for desired length, thread over twice, insert in 5th st from hook, * work off two loops, thread over, skip 2 sts, insert in next st and work off all loops on needle 2 at a time, ch 2, d c in center to complete cross. Thread over twice, insert in next st and repeat from *.

No. 15—Cluster Stitch. Work 3 or 4 tr c in same st always retaining the last loop of each tr c on needle, thread over and pull through all loops on needle.

No. 16—Lacet St. Ch for desired length, work 1 s c in 10th st from hook, ch 3 skip 2 sts, 1 d c in next st, * ch 3, skip 2 sts, 1 s c in next st, ch 3, skip 2 sts 1 d c in next st, repeat from * to end of row, 2nd row, d c in d c, ch 5 d c in next d c.

No. 17—Knot Stitch (Sometimes Called Lovers Knot St.) Ch for desired length, * draw a ¼ inch loop on hook, thread over and pull through ch, s c in single loop of st, draw another ¼ inch loop, s c into loop, skip 4 sts, s c in next st, repeat from *. To turn make ⅜″ knots, * s c in loop at right of s c and s c in loop at left of s c of previous row, 2 knot sts and repeat from *.